THE SERMON ON THE MOUNT

The Sermon on the Mount

The Perfect Measure of the Christian Life

Frank J. Matera

LITURGICAL PRESS

Collegeville, Minnesota

www.litpress.org

Cover design by Stefan Killen Design. Cover photo © iStockphoto.

1   2   3   4   5   6   7   8   9

Library of Congress Cataloging-in-Publication Data

Matera, Frank J.
    The Sermon on the Mount : the perfect measure of the Christian life / Frank J. Matera.
        p.   cm
    Includes bibliographical references.
    ISBN 978-0-8146-3523-0 — ISBN 978-0-8146-3548-3 (ebook)
    1. Sermon on the mount—Criticism, interpretation, etc.   I. Title.

BT380.3.M38 2013
226.9'06—dc23   2012044194

Dedicated to the Parishioners of
Holy Family Parish, Davidson, Maryland,
followers of Christ in the way of discipleship,
whom I have been privileged to serve from 1990 to 2012.

Contents

Preface

The Sermon on the Mount is a classic text, by which I mean
that it can be read repeatedly without exhausting its meaning.
Exactly why this is so, I am not sure; but I suspect that it has something to do with the one who first spoke its words. In this sermon
Jesus teaches with an authority that derives from his unique relationship to God; he speaks with the authority of the Son of God.
Perhaps this is why, even though the sermon has been commented
on by numerous authors, we always find something new in it.

It was Professor Jean Giblet who first introduced me to the
Sermon on the Mount in his lectures on the Synoptic Gospels at
the University of Louvain nearly fifty years ago. Since then I have
taught the Sermon on the Mount as part of my own course on
the Synoptic Gospels for nearly thirty years, and more recently I
have taught a graduate seminar on the sermon with my colleague,
Professor William Mattison, a theologian of moral theology, who
has been exploring the ethical dimension of the sermon for several
years. That seminar taught me that the sermon can be read in
different ways. This volume is my attempt to read it in a manner
that makes it accessible to a larger audience of those who want to
know what it means for their daily life.

The theme of this book is as follows: *the Sermon on the Mount
calls us to single-minded devotion to God.* It invites us to be perfect
as God is perfect by being wholehearted and undivided in our
allegiance to God. It is a call to perfection for all Christians to

be lived out in the whole of life. It is not a new set of rules and regulations; it is a call to discipleship in light of the in-breaking kingdom of God. It is, as the subtitle of this book indicates and Augustine said long ago, the perfect measure of the Christian life.

While this book is informed by critical scholarship, I have not written it for the members of the scholarly guild, although I hope that some of them will read it. I have written it for all who seek to live the Christian life. Accordingly, I have tried to write with a sense of passion and urgency about this topic since my concern is for living rather than analyzing the Christian life. While the sermon has a long and complicated critical history that I will briefly describe in the introduction to this work, my primary concern has been to focus on what it means today. This is not to say I have forgotten or neglected what the sermon meant. But that is not my primary concern. What I wish to accomplish is quite simple: provide readers with a reading of the sermon that will enrich and nourish their lives as disciples.

I am indebted to many people who have generously taken the time to read and comment on this manuscript. Among them I single out my colleagues at the Catholic University of America: Christopher Begg, William Mattison, and Regis Armstrong, and my friend and colleague Ronald Witherup, the Superior General of the Society of Saint Sulpice. All have made important contributions to this text. Most importantly, they have encouraged me—and for this I am grateful.

Frank J. Matera
June 1, 2012
The Feast of Justin Martyr
The Catholic University of America
Washington, DC

Introduction
The Sermon on the Mount and
the Christian Life

Some years ago, I read *The Cost of Discipleship* by Dietrich Bonhoeffer, the renowned German Lutheran pastor whom the Nazis executed in the final days of the Second World War for his involvement in the plot to assassinate Adolf Hitler. The heart of that volume is Bonhoeffer's commentary on the Sermon on the Mount.[1] Although I had taught the sermon in my course on the Synoptic Gospels for many years, Bonhoeffer enabled me to hear it in a way I had never heard it before. In Bonhoeffer's commentary, Christ's call to discipleship sounded forth in a powerful way. It is that reading of Bonhoeffer's commentary that has inspired this small volume, which I hope will enable others to hear the Sermon on the Mount in a new way as well. For here, in the Sermon on the Mount, we discover an outline of what it means to follow Christ in the way of discipleship.

At the outset of his own great commentary on the Sermon on the Mount, St. Augustine writes, "If anyone piously and earnestly ponders the Discourse which Our Lord Jesus Christ delivered on the Mount—as we read in the Gospel according to Matthew—I believe that he will find therein, with regard to good morals, the perfect standard of the Christian life."[2] Since Augustine, generations of commentators have endorsed this judgment. Here is the perfect measure of the Christian life, the norm by which disciples ought to live. To be sure, there have been long and intense debates about the practicality of the sermon. Can believers really live in the way that Jesus describes in this sermon? Is Jesus presenting his disciples with a realistic ethic or with an impossible ideal?

During the medieval period some theologians distinguished between precept (what one must do) and counsel (what is recommended for those seeking to be perfect), and they assigned the sermon—or parts of it—to the realm of counsel intended for those seeking the way of perfection. In reaction to this approach, which could suggest that the sermon is not intended for all believers, Martin Luther developed his teaching on the two kingdoms (one kingdom representing the public sphere of life and the other the private sphere of life). He argued that while all Christians are bound to fulfill the sermon in the private sphere of life, they are not necessarily obligated to do all of its prescriptions in the public sphere of life where they hold particular offices such as being a soldier or magistrate. Each approach to the problem of the practicality of the sermon is partly right and partly wrong. On the one hand, the sermon is a call to perfection, but it is a call for all who follow Christ in the way of discipleship rather than a counsel for a chosen few. On the other hand, the sermon is intended for all, but its claim upon the Christian is not limited to the private life of the believer but extends to the whole of life. Put another way, *the Sermon on the Mount is a call to Christian perfection intended for every believer to be lived in every sphere of life, the public as well as the private.*

Saint Augustine understood this, as did most of the early church. It was simply assumed that this is how believers ought to live. To highlight the importance of doing the sermon, Augustine quotes from its conclusion in which Jesus tells those who have just heard his words that if they hear his words and do them they will be like a wise builder whose house was not destroyed because it was built on rock. But if they hear his words and do not do them they will be like a foolish builder whose house was utterly destroyed because it was built on sand. In other words, Jesus expects those who hear the sermon to do what he teaches.

He is not presenting an impossible ideal. Nor does he intend his sermon for a chosen few. As I will argue throughout this volume, Jesus intends the sermon for all of his disciples, without exception. It is not meant for an inner circle of disciples seeking perfection. It is intended for all who follow him on the way of discipleship. It is not a private morality limited to one's personal dealings with others; it is meant to inform the whole of life.

The Sermon on the Mount as the Norm of Discipleship

Although great crowds of people hear the sermon, Jesus delivers it to his disciples. This distinction between the crowds (who form the outer circle of those who hear the sermon) and the disciples (who form the inner circle of those who hear the sermon) is crucial for understanding how to interpret the Sermon on the Mount. Jesus delivers the sermon while seated on a mountain in the hearing of the great crowds who have been following him because of the mighty deeds he has been performing on their behalf. His teaching is not secret or esoteric. It is heard by many people, even as it is today. The sermon, however, is not directed at the crowds any more than it is directed at the world. It is spoken to those who have embraced the message of the kingdom. It is spoken to those who have responded to the call of discipleship in order to provide them with a way to live within the community of disciples who follow Jesus.

While the crowds, like the world, admire Jesus' words and are amazed at the authority with which he speaks, they do not follow him in the way of discipleship. They are hearers of the word but not doers of the word. They have heard the message of the kingdom, but they have not responded to it by becoming Jesus' disciples. Accordingly, while they find the words of the sermon attractive and powerful, they have not committed themselves to Jesus as his disciples. Consequently, they do not do the words of the sermon as Jesus intends; they do not belong to the community of his disciples.

Jesus' disciples, although characterized by "little faith," have taken the initial step. They have responded to his call. They have seen the in-breaking of the kingdom of heaven in his words and deeds, and they now belong to the community of disciples that will be the church of the risen Lord. The sermon is not an impossible ideal for them because they have entered the realm of the in-breaking kingdom of God. The sermon is not an impossible ideal because they belong to a community of like-minded disciples. The practicality of the sermon is a question only for those who are not his disciples. Apart from a community of like-minded disciples, the sermon will always be impractical and idealistic. For those who do not live in the sphere of the in-breaking kingdom of God, the realm of God's grace, the sermon will always be impractical and idealistic since the sermon is intended for disciples.

In saying this, I am not excluding others from listening to, admiring, and even learning from the sermon. But I am insisting that Jesus is not just another Hellenistic philosopher. He comes as Israel's Messiah, the one who speaks with the authority of the Son of God. In doing so, he reveals the full meaning of God's will as revealed in the Law and the Prophets. What he proclaims, then, presupposes faith in his proclamation of the in-breaking kingdom of God.

Inasmuch as Jesus embodies the sermon that he preaches, his sermon is the norm by which disciples measure themselves against Jesus. The sermon is the measure of the Christian life, the norm for discipleship. This does not mean, however, that Jesus presents a new set of rules and laws in the sermon. To view the sermon as a set of laws and rules, as if the beatitudes were to supplant the Ten Commandments, is to miss the point of Jesus' sermon. To reduce the sermon to a set of rules and laws, albeit better than the old, is to misunderstand Jesus' intent. Jesus calls disciples to single-minded devotion to God. He calls them to be perfect as God is perfect by being whole and entire in their allegiance to God. To do this, Jesus shows his disciples how to live a superior righteousness: conduct in accord with God's will because one is wholeheartedly devoted to God. The sermon teaches disciples how to do what God commands.

The sermon is not a compendium of ethics. It does not address the many complicated ethical problems that contemporary

Christians face, and yet it remains the norm of discipleship. It is the perfect measure of the Christian life because it shows disciples how Jesus lived and summons them to adapt the pattern of their life to the pattern of his life. It provides a model to imitate creatively and imaginatively, while remaining ever faithful to Jesus' words. The sermon is the norm for discipleship because it teaches disciples to live in the sphere of God's kingdom. It instructs them to do God's will with single-minded devotion to God.

The Sermon on the Mount and the Sermon on the Plain

Although I am concerned with the Sermon on the Mount as found in the Gospel according to Matthew, the Gospel of Luke also records a great sermon that is usually referred to as the Sermon on the Plain (Luke 6:20-49) because Jesus delivers it on a level plain, after coming down from a mountain where he has spent the night in prayer before choosing his twelve apostles (Luke 6:17). The two sermons are similar in many ways. Both begin with a series of beatitudes that function as an introduction to the body of the sermon, and both conclude with similar warnings about the importance of doing Jesus' words. The themes that are developed in the two sermons, however, are different. Whereas the Sermon on the Mount focuses on the need for disciples to practice a righteousness that surpasses that of the scribes and the Pharisees, the Sermon on the Plain focuses on the need for disciples to love their enemies and to refrain from judging each other. Instead of discussing topics that would have been of interest to an exclusively Jewish audience, in the Sermon on the Plain Jesus devotes its attention to topics that would have been of interest to Gentiles as well as to Jews.

The Sermon on the Plain is about one-fourth the length of the Sermon on the Mount. Consequently, it does not contain all of the material found in the Sermon on the Mount. Much of the material in the Sermon on the Mount, however, is found in other parts of the Gospel of Luke, especially the section that recounts Jesus' journey to Jerusalem (Luke 9:51–19:46). The chart below compares the two sermons. The column to the left lists the topics of the Sermon on the Mount in the order in which they occur in that sermon. The column to the right shows where the topics of the Sermon on the Mount occur in the Gospel of Luke. While many of these topics occur within the Sermon on the Plain (Luke 6:20-49), others occur in the section that recounts Jesus' journey to Jerusalem (Luke 9:51–19:46).

The Sermon on the Mount (Matt 5:3–7:27)

	Matthew	Luke	
The Beatitudes	5:3-12	6:20b-23	
Salt of the Earth	5:13	14:34-35	Journey Section
Light of the World	5:14-16	8:16	Galilean Section
Law & Prophets	5:17-20	16:16-17	Journey Section
Murder & Anger	5:21-26	12:57-59	Journey Section
Adultery	5:27-30	----	
Divorce	5:31-32	16:18	Journey Section
Oaths	5:33-37	----	
Retaliation	5:38-42	6:29-32	
Love for Enemies	5:43-48	6:27-28, 32-36	
Almsgiving	6:1-4	----	
Prayer	6:5-6	----	
Lord's Prayer	6:7-15	11:1-4	Journey Section
Fasting	6:16-18	----	
Treasure in Heaven	6:19-21	12:33-34	Journey Section
Sound Eye	6:22-23	11:34-36	Journey Section
Serving Two Masters	6:24	16:13	Journey Section
Anxiety	6:25-34	12:22-32	Journey Section
Judging Others	7:1-5	6:37-42	
Profaning the Holy	7:6	----	
God's Response to Prayer	7:7-11	11:9-13	Journey Section

Golden Rule	7:12	6:31	
Two Ways	7:13-14	13:23-24	Journey Section
Good & Bad Trees	7:15-20	6:43-46	
Saying Lord, Lord	7:21-23	6:46; 13:25-27	Journey Section
House Build on Rock	7:24-27	6:47-49	

In the chart below I have again compared the two sermons, but this time the chart lists the topics of the sermon in the order they occur in the Sermon on the Plain. It shows that except for the four woes (Luke 6:24-26) all of the material in the Sermon on the Plain has a parallel in the Sermon on the Mount.

The Sermon on the Plain (Luke 6:17-49)

	Luke	Matthew
The Beatitudes	6:20b-23	5:3-12
The Woes	6:24-26	———
Love for Enemies	6:27-36	6:38-48
Judging Others	6:37-42	7:1-5
Good & Bad Trees	6:43-45	7:15-20; 12:33-35
House Built on Rock	6:46-49	7:21-27

These two charts indicate that even though the Sermon on the Mount is much longer than the Sermon on the Plain, most of the material in the Sermon on the Mount can be found in the Gospel of Luke, if not in the Sermon on the Plain then in the section that recounts Jesus' journey to Jerusalem. This difference between the two sermons raises a series of questions. Why are there two sermons? Did Jesus deliver two different sermons? Does the present form of each sermon originate with Jesus, or did Matthew and Luke play a role in the composition of the two sermons?

The questions I have posed require careful investigation, and the results of such research are often hypothetical and disputed.

Most contemporary scholars, however, would acknowledge that the content of the two sermons has its origin in the teaching of Jesus. They would also acknowledge that Matthew played an important role in the composition of the Sermon on the Mount and Luke in the composition of the Sermon on the Plain. So how did the two sermons come about? Why do we have two different sermons?

I offer the following hypothesis, to which you need not subscribe in order to read this book. First, Jesus preached about the kingdom of God on a regular basis. On certain occasions he preached memorable sermons about the ethical demands of the kingdom, which his disciples remembered. Next, after his death and resurrection, in the period before the gospels were written, the church handed on his teaching orally. That teaching took on specific forms as it was used in the catechetical and liturgical life of the church. Finally the evangelists, Matthew and Luke, employed this material in the composition of their gospels. In doing so they shaped the material to respond to their needs. Matthew, for example, organized the sermon around the themes of righteousness and the Law. His concern was to show that Jesus did not come to abolish the Law and the Prophets but to fulfill them. Luke too was interested in showing that Jesus fulfilled all that the Law and the Prophets had said about the Messiah, but he was also concerned with the great reversal that the kingdom of God was bringing. Accordingly, he balanced the four beatitudes with four woes to show that those who are first will be last, and those who are last will be first when the kingdom arrives. Luke was also interested in the demands of love, especially love for foreigners, as can be seen in the parable of the Good Samaritan. Accordingly, the body of his sermon focuses on the need to extend love to all, even to one's enemy. Thus each evangelist shaped the sermon to the needs of his audience.

Does this mean that the sermons are the compositions of the evangelists rather than of Jesus? The answer is both yes and no. Yes, the present form of each sermon is indebted to the particular evangelist who wrote the gospel. No, the content and the material of each sermon belong to Jesus rather than to the evangelists. Put another way, if we could ask Matthew and Luke if the sermon belongs to them or to Jesus, I suspect they would be surprised by the question and answer as follows: "To Jesus, of course! He is the one who spoke the words. The ideas and the concepts are his. My role was to gather the material and organize it in a way that would make it accessible and understandable to those who read my gospel." This is how I will approach the Sermon on the Mount. The present literary composition of the sermon is indebted to Matthew, but the ideas, the spirit, and the content of the sermon belong to Jesus.

The Sermon on the Mount within the Gospel of Matthew

Although Jesus is at the origin of the words that we find in the Sermon on the Mount, we no longer know the historical circumstances in which he spoke them. Indeed, the words may have been spoken several times in different circumstances, each new setting giving the words a slightly different nuance. What we do know, however, is the *literary setting of the sermon.* We know where the sermon occurs in the Gospel of Matthew within the canon of the New Testament, and it is this literary and canonical setting that provides us with the appropriate context for interpreting the sermon today. If we want to understand the sermon as Matthew intended us to hear it, then, we must read it within the context of his gospel. So where does the sermon occur within the Gospel of Matthew, and what does this setting mean for its interpretation?

The Sermon on the Mount is the first of five great discourses that Jesus delivers in the Gospel of Matthew. After each of these discourses, Matthew introduces the phrase "when Jesus had finished saying these things" (Matt 7:28; 11:1; 13:53; 19:1; 26:1), thereby indicating the end of the discourse and the beginning of a new phase in Jesus' ministry. The other four discourses are Jesus' discourse when sending his disciples on mission to the lost sheep of the house of Israel (Matt 10:1-42), Jesus' parable discourse about the kingdom of heaven (Matt 13:1-52), Jesus' discourse on how his disciples should live in community with each other (Matt 18:1-35), and Jesus' discourse on the coming destruction of the temple of Jerusalem and his return at the end of the ages as the glorious Son of Man (Matt 24:1–25:46). The Sermon on the Mount (Matt 5:1–7:27) is not an isolated discourse, then, but one of five great teachings that Jesus delivers to his disciples to prepare them for ministry. Nonetheless, the Sermon on the Mount is the most important of the five discourses, the quintessential sermon that has captured the imagination of believers. It is not by chance, then, that this is the first of Jesus' five great discourses and that it occurs at the beginning of his ministry.

The sermon comes after a long section (1:1–4:16) in which Matthew introduces Jesus to his audience so that there will be no mistake about Jesus' identity. In the Infancy Narrative (1:1–2:23), Matthew shows that Jesus is the climax of Israel's history, the son of Abraham, the son of David, the long-awaited Messiah born of the virgin through the power of God's Spirit. He is "Emmanuel," the one in whom God is present to his people, the one who will save his people from their sins. Jesus is the "king of the Jews," the one whom the Gentiles—represented by the Magi—already worship, the ruler and shepherd of God's people. He is the one who relives the history of his people by fleeing into Egypt, the Son whom God calls out of Egypt.

In the stories dealing with the preaching of John the Baptist, Jesus' baptism and testing in the wilderness, Matthew indicates that Jesus is the one who has come to fulfill all righteousness (Matt 3:15), a major theme of the Sermon on the Mount. At Jesus' baptism, the heavenly voice declares, "This is my Son, the Beloved, with whom I am well pleased" (Matt 3:17). Jesus is the obedient Son of God who, unlike Israel in the wilderness, does not fail when tested because he trusts in the power of God to save him (Matt 4:1-11). He is the light that shines upon those who dwell in darkness (Matt 4:16).

After this extended introduction in which Matthew presents Jesus as the Messiah, the Son of God, Jesus begins his ministry by proclaiming the in-breaking of God's rule, the kingdom of heaven, and calling his first disciples (Matt 4:16-22). He then teaches in the synagogues of Galilee, proclaiming the good news of the kingdom, curing every disease and sickness of his people. Great crowds from Galilee, the Decapolis, Jerusalem, Judea, and beyond the Jordan follow him (Matt 4:23). When Jesus delivers the Sermon on the Mount, then, there is no doubt about the identity and authority of the one who proclaims the sermon. He preaches the Sermon on the Mount in his capacity as Israel's long-awaited Messiah, the Son of God with whom the Father is well pleased, the one who comes to fulfill all righteousness, the one who announces the in-breaking of the kingdom of God.

Immediately after the sermon, which occurs in chapters 5–7, Matthew recounts a series of mighty deeds in chapters 8–9 that Jesus performs on behalf of Israel because the kingdom of heaven is making its appearance in his person. These mighty deeds show that the one who speaks with the authority of God is powerful in deed as well as in word. After Jesus has shown himself to be powerful in word (chaps. 5–7) and deed (chaps. 8–9), he sends his disciples on mission to the lost sheep of the house of Israel (Matt 10:5-6). The disciples are now ready for this mission because they have heard Jesus' great sermon and witnessed his mighty deeds. The literary context of the sermon, then, can be summarized in this way.

1:1–4:16   Jesus is the Messiah, the Son of God
4:17-22   Jesus proclaims the kingdom and *calls his first disciples*
4:23-25   *Summary of Jesus' teaching, preaching, and healing*
5:1–7:29   Jesus is powerful in word: Sermon on the Mount
8:1–9:34   Jesus is powerful in deed: Ten Mighty Deeds
9:35   *Summary of Jesus' teaching, preaching, and healing*
9:36-38   Jesus has compassion on the crowds
10:1-42   Jesus *sends his disciples on mission*
11:1   *Summary of Jesus' teaching and preaching*

In light of the literary context of the sermon, I make three points. First, the manner in which Matthew begins his gospel explicitly identifies Jesus as the Messiah, the Son of God. Consequently, when we come to the sermon there is no doubt about the identity of the one who speaks. Jesus delivers this sermon in his capacity as the messianic Son of God. Second, the sermon occurs shortly after Jesus' initial proclamation of the kingdom of heaven, thereby indicating that it is intimately related to his proclamation of the in-breaking kingdom. The sermon is an ethic for the kingdom of God. Apart from the kingdom, it makes little sense. Third, the sermon occurs soon after Jesus calls his first disciples, and shortly before he sends them on mission to the lost sheep of the house of Israel, thereby indicating that the sermon is intended for disciples. The sermon is an ethic of discipleship, then, that makes little sense apart from discipleship. Accordingly, as we read through the sermon it is important to remember *who* is delivering the sermon: Jesus the Messiah, the Son of God. It is important to remember *why* Jesus delivers the sermon: the kingdom of heaven is making its appearance in his ministry. Finally, it is important to remember *for whom* the sermon is intended: Jesus' disciples. Thus, Jesus the Messiah, the Son of God, delivers this sermon to his disciples in light of the in-breaking kingdom of God. If we remember these three points, there will be no question about the authority or the practicality of the sermon. The sermon is authoritative because of the one who delivers it, and it is eminently practical because it is intended for disciples who live in the sphere of God's rule.

The Structure and Theme of the Sermon on the Mount

Jesus' great sermon is a rhetorically powerful piece that argues for—and summons disciples to practice—a greater righteousness. This greater righteousness is the central theme of the sermon around which all else revolves. To appreciate the rhetoric of the sermon, however, we must pay attention to its structure and organization. The manner in which I have organized my reading of the sermon is as follows:

The Introduction to the Sermon (5:3-16)
The blessings of the kingdom: the Beatitudes (5:3-12)
The nature of discipleship: the metaphors of salt and
light (5:13-16)

The Body of the Sermon: Three Teachings on Righteousness (5:17–7:12)
Introduction: Fulfilling the Law and the Prophets (5:17-20)
Righteousness in doing the Mosaic Law (5:21-48)
Righteousness in practicing almsgiving, prayer,
fasting (6:1-18)
Righteousness as single-minded service to God
(6:19–7:11)
Conclusion: Fulfilling the Law and the Prophets (7:12)

The Conclusion to the Sermon (7:13-27)
The two ways (7:13-14)
The danger of false prophets (7:15-23)
The two builders (7:24-27)

The structure of the sermon indicates that its central theme is righteousness: conduct that accords with God's will. The righteousness that Jesus requires is a righteousness that surpasses that of the scribes and Pharisees inasmuch as it summons disciples to be perfect as their heavenly Father is perfect. To be perfect as their heavenly Father is perfect, disciples must be single-minded in their devotion to God. Accordingly, in his first teaching on righteousness, Jesus instructs the disciples how to observe the Law. In the second he shows them how to practice their piety, and in the third he explains what it means to be single-minded in devotion to God. Before beginning his teaching on righteousness, however, Jesus pronounces the blessings of the kingdom and reminds his disciples of their importance for the life of the world, thereby placing his demands for righteousness under the grace of the kingdom and the rubric of discipleship. Finally, he concludes the sermon by telling his disciples that they must be doers of the word and not merely hearers of the word, lest they enter through the wide gate and travel the broad path that leads to destruction.

The Text of the Sermon on the Mount

The Sermon on the Mount is a carefully structured text that is rhetorically powerful. In order to provide the readers of this volume with some indication of its rhetorical power, I have reproduced the text of the sermon according to the translation of the New Revised Standard Version in a way that seeks to highlight the rhetorical structure of the sermon.

The Setting of the Sermon (5:1-2)

When Jesus saw the **crowds**,
> he went up the mountain;
> and after he sat down,
> his **disciples** came to him.

Then he began to speak, and taught them, saying:

The Introduction to the Sermon (5:3-16)

The Blessings of the Kingdom: The Beatitudes (5:3-12)

Blessed are the poor in spirit,
> **for theirs is the kingdom of heaven**.

Blessed are those who mourn,
> for they will be comforted.

Blessed are the meek,
> for they will inherit the earth.

Blessed are those who hunger and thirst **for righteousness**,
> for they will be filled.

Blessed are the merciful,
> for they will receive mercy.

Blessed are the pure in heart,
> for they will see God.

Blessed are the peacemakers,
>for they will be called children of God.

Blessed are those who are persecuted **for righteousness' sake**,
>**for theirs is the kingdom of heaven**.

Blessed are **you** when people revile **you**
>>and persecute **you**
>>and utter all kinds of evil against **you** falsely
>>on my account.

Rejoice and be glad,
>for **your** reward is great in heaven,
>>for in the same way they persecuted the prophets who
>>were before **you**.

The Nature of Discipleship: The Metaphors of Salt and Light (5:13-16)

You are the **salt** of the **earth**;
>but if **salt** has lost its taste,
>>how can its saltiness be restored?
>It is no longer good for anything,
>>but is thrown out and trampled under foot.

You are the **light** of the **world**.
>A city built on a hill cannot be hid.
>No one after lighting a lamp puts it under the bushel basket,
>but on the lampstand,
>and it gives **light** to all in the house.

In the same way, let your **light** shine before others,
>so that they may see your **good works**
>and give glory to your Father in heaven.

The Body of the Sermon: Three Teachings on Righteousness (5:17–7:12)

Introduction: Fulfilling the Law and the Prophets (5:17-20)

Do not think that I have come **to abolish the law or the prophets**;
>>I have come **not to abolish**
>>>**but to fulfill**.

For truly I tell you,
> **until** heaven and earth pass away,
>> not one letter,
>> not one stroke of a letter,
>> will pass from the law
> **until** all is accomplished.

Therefore, whoever **breaks** one of the **least** of these commandments,
> and **teaches** others to do the same,
> will be called **least** in the kingdom of heaven;

but whoever **does** them
> and **teaches** them
> will be called **great** in the kingdom of heaven.

For I tell you, **unless your righteousness exceeds** that of the
scribes and Pharisees,
> you will never enter the kingdom of heaven.

The First Teaching on Righteousness: Righteousness in Doing the Mosaic Law (5:21-48)

You have heard that it was said to those of ancient times,
> 'You shall not murder'; and
> 'whoever murders shall be liable to judgment.'

But I say to you that
> **if** you are angry with a brother or sister,
>> you will be liable to judgment;
> **and if** you insult a brother or sister,
>> you will be liable to the council;
> **and if** you say, 'You fool,'
>> you will be liable to the hell of fire.

So when you are offering your gift at the altar,
> **if** you remember that your brother or sister has something
> against you,
>> **leave your gift** there before the altar and go;
>> **first be reconciled** to your brother or sister,
>> and **then come** and offer your gift.

Come to terms quickly with your accuser while you are on the
way to court with him,

or your accuser may hand you over to the judge,
>> and the judge to the guard,
>>> and you will be thrown into prison.
Truly I tell you, you will never get out until you have paid the
last penny.

You have heard that it was said,
> 'You shall not commit **adultery.**'
But I say to you that
>> everyone who looks at a woman with lust
>> has already committed **adultery** with her in his heart.
If your right eye causes you to sin,
>> **tear it out** and throw it away;
>> **it is better** for you to lose one of your members
>> **than for your whole body to be thrown into hell.**
And if your right hand causes you to sin,
>> **cut it off** and throw it away;
>> **it is better** for you to lose one of your members
>> **than for your whole body to go into hell.**

It was also said,
> 'Whoever divorces his wife, let him give her a certificate of
>> divorce.'
But I say to you that
>> anyone who divorces his wife,
>>> except on the ground of unchastity,
>> causes her to commit **adultery;**
>> and whoever marries a divorced woman commits **adultery.**

Again, you have heard that it was said to those of ancient times,
> "You shall not swear falsely,
>> but carry out the vows you have made to the Lord.'
But I say to you,
>> **Do not swear at all,**
>>> either by heaven,
>>>> for it is the throne of God,

or by the earth,
> for it is his footstool,

or by Jerusalem,
> for it is the city of the great King.

And **do not swear** by your head,
> for you cannot make one hair white or black.

Let your word be 'Yes, Yes' or 'No, No';
> anything more than this comes from the evil one.

You have heard that it was said,
> 'An eye for an eye and a tooth for a tooth.'

But I say to you,
> **Do not** resist an evildoer.
> **But if** anyone strikes you on the right cheek,
> > turn the other also;
>
> **and if** anyone wants to sue you and take your coat,
> > give your cloak as well;
>
> **and if** anyone forces you to go one mile,
> > go also the second mile.
>
> **Give** to everyone who begs from you,
> and **do not refuse** anyone who wants to borrow from you.

You have heard that it was said,
> 'You shall love your neighbor
> and hate your enemy.'

But I say to you,
> **Love** your enemies
> and **pray** for those who persecute you,
> so that you may be children of your Father in heaven;
> > for he makes his sun rise on the evil and on the good,
> > and sends rain on the righteous and on the unrighteous.

For if you love those who love you,
> **what** reward do you have?
> **Do not even** the tax collectors do the same?

And if you greet only your brothers and sisters,
> **what** more are you doing than others?
> **Do not even** the Gentiles do the same?

Be **perfect**, therefore,
> as your heavenly Father is **perfect**.

The Second Teaching on Righteousness: Righteousness in Practicing Almsgiving, Prayer, and Fasting (5:21-48)

Beware of practicing your piety before others in order to be
> seen by them;
>> for then you have no reward from your Father in heaven.

So whenever you give alms,
> **do not** sound a trumpet before you,
>> as the hypocrites do in the synagogues and in the streets,
>> so that they may be praised by others.

Truly I tell you, they have received their reward.
But when you give alms,
> do not let your **left hand** know
> what your **right hand** is doing,
> so that your alms may be done **in secret**;
>> **and your Father who sees in secret will reward you.**

And whenever you pray,
> **do not** be like the hypocrites;
>> for they love to stand and pray in the synagogues and at
>>> the street corners,
>> so that they may be seen by others.

Truly I tell you, they have received their reward.
But whenever you pray,
> go into your room and shut the door
> and pray to your Father who is **in secret**;
>> **and your Father who sees in secret will reward you.**

When you are praying,
> do not heap up empty phrases as the Gentiles do;
>> for they think that they will be heard because of their
>>> many words.

Do not be like them,
> for your Father knows what you need before you ask him.

Pray then in this way:

> Our Father in heaven,
>> hallowed be **your name**.
>>
>> **Your kingdom** come.
>>
>> **Your will** be done, on earth as it is in heaven.
>
>> **Give us** this day our daily bread.
>>
>> And **forgive us** our debts,
>>> as we also have forgiven our debtors.
>>
>> And **do not bring us** to the time of trial,
>>> but **rescue us** from the evil one.

For if you forgive others their trespasses,
> your heavenly Father will also forgive you;

but if you do not forgive others,
> neither will your Father forgive your trespasses.

And whenever you fast,
> do not look dismal, like the hypocrites,
>> for they disfigure their faces so as to show others that they are fasting.

Truly I tell you, they have received their reward.

But when you fast,
> put oil on your head and wash your face,
> so that your fasting may be seen not by others but by your Father who is **in secret**;

and your Father who sees in secret will reward you.

The Third Teaching on Righteousness: Righteousness as Single-Minded Service to God (6:19–7:11)

Do not store up for yourselves treasures on earth,
> **where** moth and rust consume and
> **where** thieves break in and steal;

but store up for yourselves treasures in heaven,
> **where** neither moth nor rust consumes and
> **where** thieves do not break in and steal.

For **where** your treasure is,

there your heart will be also.

The eye is the lamp of the body.
>So, if your eye is **healthy**,
>your whole body will be **full of light**;
>but if your eye is **unhealthy**,
>your whole body will be **full of darkness.**
>If then the light in you is **darkness**,
>how great is the **darkness**!

No one can serve two masters;
>for a slave will either hate **the one**
>and love **the other**,
>or be devoted to **the one**
>and despise **the other**.
>You cannot serve **God**
>>and **wealth.**

Therefore I tell you, **do not worry** about your life,
>what you will **eat** or
>what you will **drink**, or
>about your body,
>what you will **wear**.

Is not life more than food,
and the body more than clothing?
Look at the birds of the air;
>they neither sow nor reap nor gather into barns,
>and yet your heavenly Father feeds them.

Are you not of more value than they?
And can any of you by worrying add a single hour to your span
>of life?
And why do you worry about clothing?
Consider the lilies of the field, how they grow;
>they neither toil nor spin,
>yet I tell you, even Solomon in all his glory was not
>>clothed like one of these.
But if God so clothes the grass of the field,
>which is alive today and tomorrow is thrown into the oven,
>will he not much more clothe you—you of little faith?

Therefore **do not worry**, saying,
> 'What will we **eat**?' or
> 'What will we **drink**?' or
> 'What will we **wear**?'

For it is the Gentiles who strive for all these things;
> and indeed your heavenly Father knows that you need all
> these things.
>
> **But strive first for the kingdom of God and his
> righteousness,**
>
> and all these things will be given to you as well.

So **do not worry** about tomorrow,
> for tomorrow will bring worries of its own.
> Today's trouble is enough for today.

Do not judge,
> so that you may not be **judged**.
> For with the judgment you make
> > you will be **judged**,
> and the **measure** you give
> > will be the **measure** you get.

Why do you see the **speck** in your neighbor's **eye**,
> but do not notice the **log** in your own **eye**?

Or how can you say to your neighbor,
> 'Let me take the **speck** out of your **eye**'
> while the **log** is in your own **eye**?

You hypocrite,
> first take the **log** out of your own **eye**,
> and then you will see clearly to take the **speck** out of your
> neighbor's **eye**.

Do not give what is holy to dogs;

and do not throw your pearls before swine,
> or they will trample them under foot
> and turn and maul you.

Ask,
> and it will be given you;

search,
> and you will find;

knock,
> and the door will be opened for you.

For everyone who **asks**
> receives,

and everyone who **searches**
> finds,

and for everyone who **knocks**,
> the door will be opened.

Is there anyone among you who,
>> if your child asks for bread,
>>> will give a stone?
>> Or if the child asks for a fish,
>>> will give a snake?

If you then, who are evil, know how to give good gifts to your children,
>> **how much more** will your Father in heaven give good things to those who ask him!

Conclusion: Fulfilling the Law and the Prophets (7:12)

In everything do to others as you would have them do to you;
> **for this is the law and the prophets.**

Conclusion to the Sermon (7:13-27)

The Two Ways (7:13-14)

Enter through the narrow gate;
> **for the gate** is wide
>> and **the road** is easy that leads to destruction,
>> and there are **many** who take it.

> **For the gate** is narrow
>> and **the road** is hard that leads to life,
>> and there are **few** who find it.

The Danger of False Prophets (7:15-23)

Beware of false prophets,
>who come to you in **sheep's clothing**
>but inwardly are **ravenous wolves**.

You will know them by their **fruits**.
>Are grapes gathered from thorns,
>or figs from thistles?

In the same way, every **good tree** bears **good fruit**,
but the **bad tree** bears **bad fruit**.
A **good tree** cannot bear **bad fruit**,
nor can a **bad tree** bear **good fruit**.
Every **tree** that does not bear **good fruit** is cut down and
>thrown into the fire.

Thus you will know them by their **fruits**.

The Two Builders (7:24-27)

Not everyone who says to me, '**Lord, Lord**,' will enter the king-
>dom of heaven,
>>but only the one who does the will of my Father in heaven.

On that day many will say to me, '**Lord, Lord,**
>did we not prophesy in your name,
>and cast out demons in your name,
>and do many deeds of power in your name?'

I will declare to them,
>'I never knew you; go away from me, you evildoers.'

Everyone then who **hears** these words of mine and **acts on them**
>will be like a **wise man**
>who **built his house on rock**.
>>The rain fell,
>>the floods came,
>>and the winds blew and beat on that house,
>>but it did not fall, because it had been **founded on rock**.

And everyone who **hears** these words of mine and **does not act
on them**
>will be like a **foolish man**
>who **built his house on sand**.

The rain fell,
and the floods came,
and the winds blew and beat against that house,
and it fell—and great was its fall!

The Reaction of the Crowds to the Sermon (7:28-29)

Now when Jesus had finished saying these things,
the **crowds** were **astounded** at his teaching,
for he taught them **as one having authority**,
and not as their scribes.

Notes

1. Dietrich Bonhoeffer, *The Cost of Discipleship,* trans. R. H. Fuller (New York: Simon & Schuster, 1995), 103–97.

2. *Commentary on the Lord's Sermon on the Mount with Seventeen Related Sermons,* trans. Denis J. Kavanaugh, OSA, The Fathers of the Church 11 (Washington, DC: The Catholic University of America Press, 1951).

The Blessings of the Kingdom and the Nature of Discipleship

The Christian moral life is not a matter of observing rules and regulations, although it often appears that way. It is a life lived in response to God's grace; it is a life made possible by the new life believers have received from God in Christ through the power of the Holy Spirit. Thus the nature of Christian obedience—what Paul calls the obedience of faith—is rooted in the gift of salvation. Believers strive to live in a particular way because of the gift of salvation that God has given them in Christ.

Whereas the Pauline letters express this gift in terms of the Spirit, the Synoptic Gospels focus on the salvation the kingdom of God has inaugurated. The kingdom that Jesus proclaimed, and into which he entered by his saving death and life-giving resurrection, opens a new sphere where believers can live in a new way. No longer under the power and rule of Satan, those who embrace the kingdom have entered the realm of God's rule where all things are possible. Having turned from the rule of the one who brings them to sin and death, they have embraced a new way of life made possible by the gift of the kingdom, which is nothing less than God's rule over their lives. This is why Jesus' Sermon on the Mount begins with a series of blessings that assure his disciples of the final beatitude that will be theirs when the kingdom is revealed in all of its power. This is why it is only after he proclaims the salvation the kingdom brings that Jesus presents the demands of the new life that define the behavior of those who embrace God's rule over their lives. Accordingly, while the sermon is filled with ethical demands, it begins with the blessings of the kingdom (the beatitudes) that reveal the new life Jesus' disciples have begun to enjoy, and will enjoy in its fullness at the end of the ages. It is from this perspective of salvation that I consider the preamble to the sermon: the beatitudes and the metaphors of salt and light (5:3-16). Before doing so, however, it is important to say something about the audience of the Sermon on the Mount.

The Disciples and the Crowds (5:1-2)

Matthew situates the Sermon on the Mount at the start of Jesus' ministry, shortly after he begins his preaching about the kingdom of heaven and calls his first disciples (Matt 4:17-22). The immediate upshot of Jesus' ministry is that people come to him from all the surrounding regions in order to be healed (Matt 4:23-25). Seeing the great crowds that approach him, Jesus goes up a mountain where he sits; his disciples come to him, and he teaches them in the hearing of the crowds. The mountain, then, functions like a pulpit from which Jesus instructs his disciples in the presence of the large crowds that have followed him.

Although the precise location and meaning of the mountain are not specified, it functions as a place of revelation from which Jesus teaches in his capacity as the Son of God with an authority that amazes the crowds. This setting continues to play an important role in the rest of the gospel. For example, Jesus ascends the mountain and is seated when large crowds come to him to be healed (Matt 15:29-31); he ascends a very high mountain where he is transfigured before Peter, James, and John (Matt 17:1-8); and after his resurrection he summons his disciples to the mountain in Galilee where he commissions them to preach the gospel to the whole world (Matt 28:16-20).

But who is Jesus teaching? To be sure, the crowds as well as his disciples hear this sermon. The setting of the sermon, however, suggests that the disciples rather than the crowds are Jesus' immediate audience, the inner circle to whom he speaks, whereas the crowds form the outer circle of his audience. The crowds will hear the sermon, but Jesus' primary aim is to teach his disciples to whom he will give a share in his authority and send on mission to the lost sheep of the house of Israel (Matt 10:6). Whereas the crowds represent Israel, the disciples are the first fruits of the renewal and restoration of Israel. The disciples have already heard Jesus' initial preaching about the in-breaking kingdom and repented. They have heard his proclamation of the dawning rule of God and left everything to follow him. In addressing his teaching to the disciples, Jesus announces the blessings of the kingdom that will be theirs and describes the higher conduct—the greater righteousness—that must characterize their lives. The crowds will hear this teaching, and many will be attracted to it. For some it will lead to a moment of conversion and renewal; for others it will be too harsh, and they will no longer follow the one who has healed their ills. But for Jesus' disciples, the sermon will be a decisive moment in their lives, defining what it means to be a disciple, describing how to live as a disciple, promising the disciples the beatitude that will be theirs.

The setting of the Sermon on the Mount, then, separates the disciples from the crowds, the Christian from the world, the believer from the unbeliever. Whereas the world hears the sermon with curiosity, interest, admiration, and even approval, it sees no need to follow the one who teaches these words. It examines his words, discusses his teaching, debates what he says, agreeing with some things and disregarding others, but it sees no need to obey his precepts—at least not all of them. The world is free to pick, to choose, and to decide what it will accept and reject. But this is not so for Jesus' disciples; this is not so for those who hear these words in faith. For the disciples and those who will hear these words with a pure heart, they are the teaching of the one who proclaims and inaugurates the kingdom of heaven. They are the words of the Messiah, the Son of God. They are not words to be dissected and analyzed, but words to be lived and obeyed. This is why Jesus directs his sermon to his disciples; for only those who believe in the dawning of the kingdom and the one who proclaims it can understand the sermon from the point of view of the one who teaches it. Only they can grasp its meaning, not because they possess superior insight or intelligence, but because they have been chosen and elected to hear, to obey, and to live its words.

The Disciples' Assurance of Beatitude (5:3-12)

Jesus begins his teaching with a series of statements that pronounce a blessing upon certain people. But who are they? And what is the nature of this blessing? Are these statements a series of ethical maxims that people must obey in order to enter the kingdom of heaven? Or are they a series of statements that assure those who belong to the kingdom of the final beatitude that will be theirs when the kingdom appears in all its power and glory? The position I will develop can be summarized in this way: *the ethical content of the beatitudes must be interpreted in light of the final beatitude that Jesus promises his disciples.* Instead of viewing the beatitudes as a set of rules and regulations, then, I will present them as a description of the beatitude that Jesus promises disciples who have embraced the kingdom of heaven, the rule of God over their lives. In affirming this, I am not denying or downplaying the ethical content of the beatitudes, but seeking the proper vantage point from which to describe that content so that the demands of the sermon will be grounded in the salvation the kingdom brings.

Although we are accustomed to speak of the eight beatitudes, there are in fact nine, the first eight expressed in the third person plural ("blessed are *the . . .*"), and the ninth in the second person plural ("blessed are *you*"), thereby providing a smooth transition to the metaphors of salt and light, which are also expressed in the second person plural ("*you* are the salt/light of the earth"). But in addition to providing a transition to the metaphors of salt and light, the use of the second person plural reveals that the first eight beatitudes are, in fact, addressed to the disciples. Therefore, while the first eight beatitudes appear to be framed as general maxims, the ninth beatitude shows that they are addressed to the disciples sitting before Jesus on the mountain.

Each of the beatitudes has two parts. In the first part, Jesus pronounces a blessing on certain people ("blessed are the poor in spirit"). In the second, he provides the reason for this blessing ("because theirs is the kingdom of God"). Those over whom Jesus pronounces the blessing are not blessed simply because of some ethical quality they have attained, however, but because of the final or eschatological blessing that God will bring about in their lives. Their blessedness or happiness, then, is not so much the result of their own effort as it is the result of the gift of final salvation that God brings with the kingdom.

The way in which the first eight beatitudes are set off from the ninth beatitude suggests that the first eight can be divided into two parts. Thus, whereas the eschatological blessing of the first and the eighth beatitude is *for theirs is the kingdom of heaven*, the subjects of the fourth and the eighth beatitudes are those who hunger and thirst for *righteousness* and are persecuted for their *righteousness*, respectively. Accordingly, references to the kingdom of heaven (the central content of Jesus' preaching) set the limits for the first eight beatitudes, and references to righteousness (the theme of the sermon) divide the first eight beatitudes into two groups of four. The very structure of the beatitudes, then, points to its central blessing and ethical content: the kingdom of heaven and the righteousness appropriate to it.

> Blessed are the poor in spirit
> **for theirs is kingdom of heaven**
> Blessed are those who mourn
> for they will be comforted
> Blessed are the meek
> for they will inherit the earth
> Blessed are those who hunger and thirst **for**
> **righteousness**
> for they will be satisfied

> Blessed are the merciful
>> for they will receive mercy
>
> Blessed are the pure in heart
>> for they will see God
>
> Blessed are the peacemakers
>> for they will be called children of God
>
> Blessed are those who are persecuted **for**
> **righteousness' sake**
>> **for theirs is the kingdom of heaven**

Although Jesus pronounces eight beatitudes, he does not address eight categories of people. The beatitudes describe those who belong to the kingdom and, as we shall see, they describe the one who proclaims the sermon. Accordingly, the poor in spirit are those who mourn, those who are meek, those who hunger and thirst for righteousness. It is they who will be comforted, inherit the earth, and be satisfied when they enter the fullness of the kingdom. Although Jesus describes those who are blessed and assures them of beatitude in different ways, he is describing all who have embraced the kingdom and wait for its final manifestation.

Blessed are the poor in spirit (5:3). The background to this beatitude, and indeed to all of the beatitudes, is the prophecy of Isaiah 61 that Jesus fulfills through his ministry (Luke 4:16-21).

> The spirit of the Lord God is upon me, because the LORD has anointed me; he has sent me **to bring good news to the oppressed**, to bind up the brokenhearted, to proclaim liberty to the captives, and release to the prisoners; to proclaim the year of the LORD's favor, and the day of vengeance of our God; **to comfort all who mourn**; to provide for **those who mourn in Zion**—to give them a garland instead of ashes, the oil of gladness instead of mourning, the mantle of praise instead of a faint spirit. They will be called **oaks of righteousness**, the planting of the LORD, to display his glory. (Isa 61:1-3)

The good news that Jesus brings to the poor in spirit is that the kingdom of heaven is making its appearance, and when it arrives there will be a reversal of fortunes whereby many who are first will be last, and many who are last will be first. For the poor and oppressed who find themselves on the margins of society, ignored and overlooked by the powerful, this is good news. But who are these poor whom Jesus has in view? They are Jesus' disciples who have believed in his gospel of the kingdom and left everything to follow him. They are the disciples sitting before him and listening to his teaching. They are the men and women of every age who embrace the kingdom of heaven in order to follow Christ as his disciples.

But why does Jesus describe them as "poor in spirit"? Why not simply call them "the poor"? This added description, over which interpreters have puzzled, does not mean that Jesus has spiritualized the meaning of poverty. After all, the disciples who have responded to his call are truly poor; they have left family and livelihood to follow him. This is why Peter says that he and the other disciples have left everything to follow Jesus (Matt 19:27). But poverty of itself is not enough; for even the poor can be mean-spirited. By describing his disciples as poor *in spirit,* Jesus points to their relationship with God. Their poverty has touched their inmost being so that they now depend entirely upon God. Poor and oppressed, having left all to follow Christ, they find themselves utterly dependent upon him, and so upon God. Their poverty is a poverty that touches the deepest core of their being—it touches their spirit—making it possible for them to enjoy a new relationship with God. Because they are poor in respect to their inmost being, they depend upon God in a way they could not and did not before. Is such poverty of spirit possible for those who are rich and affluent? Yes, it is possible, but it is difficult (Matt 19:23-24). Although it is difficult, however, it is not impossible since all things are possible for God (Matt 19:26). Like the poor of Israel who looked to God as their vindicator because they had no one else upon whom to depend, the poor in spirit rely upon God alone.

And so the kingdom of heaven is theirs. What a remarkable statement, so unexpected, so contrary to our way of viewing the world. The kingdom of heaven belongs to disciples who have surrendered everything and now depend solely upon God. This kingdom is the central content of Jesus' teaching (Matt 4:17). Everything he does and says refers to the in-breaking kingdom of heaven that is making its appearance in his ministry. This kingdom, however, is not a geographical place; it is not even heaven. It is the in-breaking rule of God over the lives of those who submit to God's rule. It is God's rule over a creation gone astray, which finds itself under the power and sway of Satan. This is what Jesus comes to announce: the kingdom is making its appearance in his life and ministry, and those who wish to enter it must turn from an old way of life with which they are comfortable and familiar to a new way of life in order to enter the new creation defined by God's rule. Such a change requires faith on the part of disciples—faith that Jesus is truly the herald of the kingdom, faith that God is bringing about a new creation in and through Jesus. The kingdom already belongs to the poor in spirit inasmuch as they have submitted to God's rule by following Christ. Although the kingdom will not be present in all of its power and glory until the Son of Man returns at the end of the ages, the poor in spirit experience something of its power even now. Thus Jesus' disciples live between the ages, between what has already happened and what has yet to occur.

Blessed are those who mourn (5:4). At first it may seem strange to think of Jesus' disciples as mourning. After all, when the Pharisees ask him why his disciples do not fast, Jesus replies that the wedding guests, his disciples, *cannot mourn* so long as he, the bridegroom, is with them (Matt 9:15). What Jesus' disciples do mourn, however, is the continuing power of sin and death in the world. Like those who mourned in Zion because of the humiliation and destruction that Jerusalem endured at the time of the Exile, the disciples mourn that they are in exile so long as the old age prevents the new age from breaking in. They do not mourn for personal loss and injury, as great as such injury and loss may be. They mourn for what has happened to God's people. And yes, as sinful human beings, they mourn for the disgrace that has come upon God's name because of their sins. Those who mourn, however, do so in hope of the final appearance of the kingdom that will fulfill the promises God has made to his people.

Those who think of salvation in merely personal terms (the salvation of *my* soul) do not understand the full meaning of this beatitude, which has in view the wider community of believers. Thus, whereas those in Zion wept for the national tragedy that befell Israel at the time of the Babylonian captivity, contemporary disciples mourn for the church that still struggles in the old age of sin and death as it waits to enter into the fullness of the new age. They mourn for the suffering and persecution that afflict the church of every age; they mourn because their sins have prevented the church from being a light to all nations.

Jesus promises that his disciples *will be comforted.* The future passive tense points to something God will do for those who mourn. While others may comfort and console the disciples, only God will be able to wipe away every tear. Those who mourn, then, are not blessed because of something they have done but because of what God will do for them when the kingdom of heaven appears in all its glory. On that day God will comfort them by destroying the enemy of all that is good. But until that day disciples will mourn, not because they are saddened by personal loss, but because they intensely long for the salvation that only the kingdom of heaven can bring: a new and restored Jerusalem in which every tear will be wiped away and God's people will live in perfect obedience to God's will.

Blessed are the meek (5:5). Jesus now describes his disciples in a way that echoes Psalm 37, which promises that the meek will inherit the land. The Psalm begins with an exhortation to the righteous "not to fret because of the wicked" or "be envious of wrongdoers," for they will quickly fade "like the grass, and wither like the green herb" (vv. 1-2). Instead, the just are to "trust in the LORD, and do good" so that they "will live in the land, and enjoy security" (v. 3). Then, on four occasions, the Psalmist employs the refrain that Jesus uses in this beatitude.

> But the meek *shall inherit the land,*
>> And delight themselves in abundant prosperity.
>> (v. 11)

> For those blessed by the LORD *shall inherit the land,*
>> but those cursed by him shall be cut off. (v. 22)

> The righteous *shall inherit the land,*
>> and live in it forever. (v. 29)

> Wait for the LORD, and keep to his way,
>> and he will exalt you *to inherit the land;*
>> you will look on the destruction of the wicked.
>> (v. 34)

At the conclusion of the Psalm, the Psalmist says, "The salvation of the *righteous* is from the LORD; . . . he rescues them from the wicked, and saves them, *because they take refuge in him*" (vv. 39-40).

For the Psalmist the meek are the righteous. Like the poor in spirit, they are the ones who take refuge in the Lord. No matter how important they may be, they are not impressed by their own importance. And so they are humble; they are gentle; they are as concerned for the needs of others as they are for their own needs. This is why, when God rises up in judgment, he saves the meek, the oppressed of the earth (Ps 76:9). This is why God lifts up the meek, casts down the wicked (Ps 147:6), and exalts the meek with salvation (Ps 149:4). This is why Moses is described as meek, "more so than anyone else on the face of the earth" (Num 12:3), for he trusted in God rather than in himself.

The model of meekness is Jesus who describes himself as meek and humble of heart (Matt 11:29). He does not come as a powerful warrior-king to establish his kingdom by power and force but as the meek and humble king whom Zechariah foretold: "mounted on a donkey, and on a colt, the foal of a donkey" (Matt 21:5, quoting Zech 9:9). Jesus is meek because he knows that it is the Lord who "overthrows the thrones of rulers, and enthrones the *meek* or the lowly in their place" (Sir 10:14; slightly modified

NRSV). Although this will be the hardest lesson for Jesus' disciples to learn—one they will consistently fail to grasp—Jesus addresses them as the meek because God is their refuge.

The land they will inherit, however, is not simply the land that the rich and powerful already occupy. If that were the case, Jesus would be just another revolutionary promising the poor their share of the land. The land his disciples will inherit is the earth that will be changed and transformed by the kingdom of God—the new heaven and the new earth that will appear at the resurrection of the dead. This is why Jesus tells his disciples that "at *the renewal of all things*, when the Son of Man is seated on the throne of his glory, you who have followed me will also sit on twelve thrones, judging the twelve tribes of Israel" (Matt 19:28).

Blessed are those who hunger and thirst for righteousness (5:6). With this beatitude Jesus introduces the theme of his sermon: the righteousness the kingdom of heaven requires. Although the concept of "righteousness" is strange to most contemporary believers, it plays a central role in Scripture where it can refer to God's own righteousness as well as to the righteousness of those who live in accordance with God's will. Understood in reference to God, it refers to God's own righteousness; that is, to God's uprightness, God's faithfulness to the covenant, God's utter reliability because God always acts with integrity, thereby assuring a just judgment. When predicated of human beings, righteousness refers to a quality and relationship with God that people enjoy when they do the righteousness that accords with God's will as revealed in the Mosaic Law: such people are righteous. The righteous, then, are those who stand in a right relationship to God because they have done God's will; they have done righteousness. God will declare such people "righteous" on the last day.

Whereas the Old Testament understands righteousness in terms of Torah observance, Paul defines it in terms of Jesus Christ. Accordingly, he presents righteousness as the saving gift God bestows on those who believe in Christ. The manner in which Jesus speaks of righteousness in the Sermon on the Mount, however, is closer to the Old Testament notion of righteousness: *righteousness is conduct that accords with God's will.* Viewed from this perspective, those who hunger and thirst for righteousness are those who seek to do God's will with all their mind, with all their heart, and with all their strength. There is nothing more important for them than to do God's will by practicing righteousness. As Jesus looks at his disciples, he knows they hunger and thirst *to do* this righteousness, even though they do not yet comprehend its full demands.

Before teaching his disciples what it means to be righteous, Jesus exemplifies righteousness in his own life by submitting to John's baptism of repentance. Jesus is the sinless Son of God, but he stands before John and asks to be baptized. Aware that Jesus is the mightier one for whom he is preparing the way, John tries to prevent him from doing so. But Jesus responds, "Let it be so now; for it is proper for us in this way to fulfill all righteousness" (Matt 3:15). By submitting to John's baptism, Jesus shows that he is the one who comes to do all righteousness; he comes to do and fulfill the law and the prophets. Before he teaches his disciples how to live righteously in a way that is pleasing to God, then, Jesus fulfills all righteousness by doing what God requires.

Jesus promises that those who hunger and thirst for righteousness *will be* satisfied. In saying this, he indicates that righteousness is an eschatological blessing that only God can bring to fulfillment. Although disciples hunger and thirst to do God's will, only God can fulfill their longing. Only God can empower them to live in a way pleasing to God. Accordingly, the fullness of a life of righteousness will only be achieved when the kingdom comes in all of its glory. In the time before the coming of the kingdom, disciples will continue to hunger and thirst to live in a way pleasing to God. They will long to live the kind of righteousness that Jesus describes in this sermon.

Blessed are the merciful (5:7). With this beatitude, Jesus invokes the law of reciprocity: disciples will receive mercy to the extent they extend mercy to others. Jesus will reinforce this principle of reciprocity when he teaches his disciples to pray by promising them that if they forgive others their heavenly Father will forgive them, and by warning them that if they do not forgive others neither will their heavenly Father forgive them (Matt 6:14-15). He will then illustrate this principle through the story of a servant who, after having been forgiven an enormous debt, refuses to forgive the small debt of a fellow servant, leading his master to say: "Should you not have had mercy on your fellow slave, as I had mercy on you?" (Matt 18:33). Disciples, then, ought to extend mercy to others because they have already experienced something of God's mercy through Jesus who calls them to follow him in the way of discipleship.

Mercy is one of the distinguishing qualities of God. In revealing himself to Moses, for example, God proclaims, "The LORD, the LORD, a God *merciful and gracious*, slow to anger, and abounding in steadfast love and faithfulness" (Exod 34:6). The Psalmist repeatedly echoes this description of God: "But you, O Lord, are a God *merciful and gracious*, slow to anger and abounding in steadfast love and faithfulness" (Ps 86:15; see also Pss 103:8; 111:4; 145:8). In pronouncing this beatitude Jesus has in view God's own mercy, which his disciples have already experienced in his proclamation of the kingdom. Those who are merciful are those who know that God is merciful, and so they are merciful to others.

Jesus exemplifies the beatitude he pronounces. When the Pharisees complain that he eats with tax collectors and sinners, and when they fault his disciples for violating the Sabbath, he cites the prophet Hosea: "Go and learn what this means, 'I desire mercy not sacrifice'" (Matt 9:13; 12:7, quoting Hos 6:6), and whenever those in need call upon him for mercy (Matt 9:27; 15:22; 20:30-31), he heals their ills. Jesus comes to Israel as the merciful Messiah who fulfills the prophecy of Isaiah: "He took our infirmities and bore our diseases" (Matt 8:17, quoting Isa 53:4). The most important matters of the law for the merciful Messiah are justice, mercy, and faith (Matt 23:23). Therefore, the mercy that people extend or fail to extend to others will be the criterion by which the Messiah will separate the sheep from the goats when he returns as the glorious Son of Man to judge the nations (Matt 25:31-46).

While the world views mercy in terms of weakness and emotion, Jesus understands it in light of the mercy that God extends to sinners and those in need. Such mercy is not an emotion; it is a quality of God. To extend mercy to others is to imitate God. This is why Jesus commands his disciples, "Be merciful, just as your Father is merciful" (Luke 6:36).

Blessed are the pure in heart (5:8). Nothing is more important than standing in the presence of God. What disciples long for is that moment when they will see God. This is why the Psalmist writes, "My soul thirsts for God, for the living God. When shall I come and behold the face of God?" (Ps 42:2). But who can stand in the presence of the all holy God without being consumed by the divine fire? Who can see God and live? Those pilgrims who journeyed to the temple of Jerusalem were deeply aware of their unworthiness to stand in God's presence, and so the Psalmist asks, "Who shall ascend the hill of the LORD? And who shall stand in his holy place?" (Ps 24:3). In response, he replies, "Those who have clean hands and *pure hearts*, who do not lift up their souls to what is false, and do not swear deceitfully" (Ps 24:4). Echoing the Psalmist, Jesus promises his disciples a still greater blessing. Whereas the Psalmist sought to stand in God's presence in the temple, Jesus promises that his disciples will *see* God when they enter the fullness of the kingdom of heaven.

But who can stand in the presence of God and live? Jesus can because he is the very Son of God, the one whom the Father sent into the world. He is the one who stood in the presence of the Father. He is the one who can say, "no one knows the Father except the Son and anyone to whom the Son chooses to reveal him" (Matt 11:27). He is the one who calls God his Father, and so he can promise the pure in heart that they will see God.

The pure in heart are single-minded in their devotion to God. They are not divided or conflicted in their allegiance to God, trying to please both God and human beings. They have only one goal and purpose—to please God, and so their heart is pure because of its undivided allegiance to God. Since their entire being is focused on God in a way that is perfect and undivided, Jesus promises they will see God.

Jesus exemplifies the beatitude by his perfect allegiance to God. When John tries to dissuade him from being baptized, he insists upon doing all righteousness (Matt 3:15). When the devil tempts Jesus to use his messianic power to save himself, Jesus trusts in God's power to rescue him (Matt 4:1-10). Rather than insisting on his own will in the Garden of Gethsemane, Jesus submits to God's will (Matt 26:39, 42); and when challenged to come down from the cross and save himself, he trusts in the power of God to save him (Matt 27:39-44). Because he is single-minded in his devotion to God, Jesus is pure in heart, perfect in his allegiance to God.

Blessed are the peacemakers (5:9). Since Jesus' disciples have already experienced the peace and reconciliation that the kingdom of God brings in the person of Jesus, they work to reconcile those who are estranged from each other. This is why, when he sends his disciples on mission, Jesus instructs them to greet whatever house they enter with an announcement of the peace the kingdom brings (Matt 10:12-13). In announcing the peace of the kingdom, Jesus' disciples anticipate the peace and reconciliation that Jesus brings "through the blood of his cross" (Col 1:20) whereby Christ created "in himself one new humanity in place of the two, thus making peace" (Eph 2:17). Those who make peace by reconciling others imitate the Son of God, and so they will be called God's sons and daughters when the kingdom arrives in power and glory.

Inasmuch as he is Israel's Messiah, Jesus is the "Prince of Peace" of whom Isaiah spoke (Isa 9:6), the one in whose days righteousness flourishes and peace abounds (Ps 72:7). The Book of the prophet Isaiah says that the effect of this righteousness will be peace (Isa 32:17), and the prophet exclaims, "How beautiful upon the mountains are the feet of the messenger who announces peace" (Isa 52:7). Jesus' disciples are messengers of peace, and so it is not surprising that Paul describes the gospel as "the gospel of peace" (Eph 6:15) and God as "the God of peace" (Rom 15:33; Phil 4:9).

Making peace requires disciples to live the law in a way that produces righteousness, which James calls the harvest of peace (Jas 3:18). As peacemakers, the disciples must avoid anger, forsake retaliation, and love their enemies (Matt 5:21-26, 38-48). As the nucleus of the new community Jesus is establishing, they must be reconciled to each other and reconcile those who have gone astray (Matt 18:10-20).

Blessed are those who are persecuted for righteousness' sake (5:10). This beatitude echoes the fourth beatitude, which Jesus addressed to those who hunger and thirst for righteousness, and it repeats the blessing of the first beatitude: the kingdom of heaven is theirs. Whereas the ninth beatitude will explicitly address the disciples ("Blessed are *you* . . .") and foretell the persecution they *will* suffer, this beatitude implies that Jesus' disciples have already experienced persecution because they have embraced the righteousness he teaches. True disciples, then, are persecuted for doing the very righteousness for which they hunger and thirst. Having been chosen and elected by Jesus, and having experienced something of the righteousness of the kingdom in the person of Jesus, they hunger and thirst to live as he lives, and the result of such a life is persecution. But the persecution of the world is not the final word, nor is it the final judgment over Jesus' disciples. The final word belongs to God. This is why Jesus promises that the kingdom belongs to those who are being persecuted for living according to its righteousness.

Once more, Jesus is the model of the beatitude he proclaims. Throughout his life and ministry, he exemplifies the righteousness of God's kingdom by living in conformity with God's will. The outcome of this life, however, is persecution that culminates in death on the cross. But it will be God and not the world that will have the final word. The persecuted Messiah—the one who suffers because he lives a righteous life—will enter the fullness of the kingdom when God raises him from the dead.

Before considering the ninth beatitude, I would like to make two points. First, although the beatitudes speak of different people and pronounce varied eschatological blessings, they find their point of unity in the one who proclaims them: Jesus the Messiah who exemplifies what he proclaims in his life. Second, although the beatitudes speak of different people and blessings, these people and blessings are essentially the same. The poor in spirit are those who mourn. They are the meek, those who hunger and thirst for righteousness. They are the merciful, the pure of heart. They are the peacemakers, those persecuted because they live righteously. Therefore the kingdom belongs to them, and because it does they will be comforted, inherit the earth, be satisfied, be shown mercy, see God, and be called sons and daughters of God. In a word, Jesus exemplifies as well as describes the perfect disciple.

Blessed are you when people revile you (5:11-12). On first hearing, this beatitude seems out of place. On the one hand, it is different in form from the first eight beatitudes. On the other, it appears to repeat what has already been said in the previous beatitude. The different form of the beatitude ("blessed are *you* . . . , rejoice and be glad . . . , for in the same way . . .*), however, serves several purposes. First, the use of the second person plural (*you*) indicates that Jesus explicitly directs this beatitude to his disciples, thereby indicating that the other beatitudes were addressed to them as well. Second, by emphasizing that the disciples will be reviled, persecuted, and spoken against falsely *on his account,* Jesus highlights the intimate relationship that exists between him and his disciples: what they suffer for the gospel they suffer for him; and what they suffer for him they suffer for the gospel. Third, the beatitude places the disciples within Israel's prophetic tradition that Jesus is presently fulfilling by proclaiming the in-breaking kingdom of heaven. The suffering of the disciples is neither unique nor isolated since Israel's prophets suffered similar revilement. And so, just as the prophets endured persecution because they proclaimed God's righteous demands, Jesus' disciples will suffer persecution for proclaiming the righteousness of the kingdom.

Suffering is not to be sought for its own sake. Of itself, it is not a positive value. Rather than encourage his disciples to seek suffering, Jesus explains the meaning of the suffering they will endure because they are his disciples. In doing so, he relates their suffering to the prophetic tradition of Israel, thereby giving it meaning and significance within the wider scope of salvation history. Such suffering is transformative because it is related to God's plan. Paul, for example, understood that by suffering for the gospel he was being conformed to the crucified Christ. Jesus' disciples must learn something similar: the persecutions they will endure are the birth pangs of the new age.

The Disciples and the World (5:13-16)

Although the world will revile and persecute the disciples for the gospel they bring, it persecutes them at its own peril; for the disciples are to the world what salt is to everyday life. The disciples are the salt of the earth inasmuch as the gospel they bring preserves the world from evil. The disciples are the salt of the earth inasmuch as the gospel they proclaim is the seasoning that gives the world its deepest meaning. The disciples are the salt of the earth inasmuch as the gospel of the kingdom is the proclamation of the new covenant, the salt of the covenant whereby humanity is reconciled to God. But if disciples cease to function as disciples, if they do not take up their cross and follow Jesus, if they proclaim the gospel in a way that accommodates it to the world rather than the world to the gospel, the disciples will no longer be the salt of the earth. If the gospel they preach is no longer a gospel about Christ, the disciples will no longer be the salt of the earth. Having forfeited what it means to be a disciple by accommodating themselves to the world, they will become like salt that has lost its ability to season and preserve. Having lost their purpose for being disciples, they will be thrown out and trampled underfoot by the very world they tried to appease by compromising the gospel.

Jesus is the light of the world (John 8:12), and through the proclamation of the kingdom he brings light to those sitting in the shadow of death (Matt 4:12-16). But now, in one of the boldest statements of the gospel, he tells his disciples that they (the very ones whom the world will hate, despise, and persecute) are the light of the world. They are not the light of the world because of their merits and deeds but because of Jesus, the Servant of God who brings the light of salvation so that God's salvation may reach to the ends of the earth (Isa 49:6). So long as disciples do what Jesus has done, therefore, they will be the light of the world, freeing the world from the darkness of sin and death.

Jesus compares his disciples to a city built on a hill. Such a city cannot be hidden. Indeed, the purpose of building it on a hill is to insure that it will be seen by others. Jesus' disciples are to be what Jerusalem was intended to be: a city that manifests the everlasting light of God to the world (Isa 60:3, 19-20). Just as the purpose of a lamp is to dispel the darkness, the purpose of being a disciple is to bring light to those in darkness. Therefore, disciples must be single-minded in their devotion to God so that they will be filled with light (Matt 6:22). Filled with the light and courage that come from the gospel, they are to proclaim in the light what they have heard in the darkness. They are to announce from the rooftop what they have heard whispered (Matt 10:27). Since the kingdom has made its appearance in Jesus' ministry, the purpose of the disciples is to proclaim what they have heard.

Inasmuch as what the disciples proclaim is the gospel, they must manifest their good works to others. Therefore, disciples are not to hide their good works but to do them in a way that others will see them. On first hearing this appears to contradict what Jesus will say when he exhorts his disciples *not* to perform their acts of piety for others to see (Matt 6:1). But whereas in that passage Jesus will criticize those who do their acts of piety to win the praise of others, here Jesus encourages his disciples to do their good works so that others will not praise them but praise their heavenly Father. To be the light of the world means to praise God by bringing the light of salvation to those in darkness.

Who are the disciples and what can they expect? On the one hand they stand in contrast to the crowds that follow Jesus. Jesus has chosen and elected the disciples from the crowds to be the nucleus of a renewed people. They stand in contrast to the world that dwells in darkness ever ready to revile and persecute them for the gospel they bring, even though it is the gospel that gives meaning to the world and dispels the darkness. On the other hand, the disciples stand in a unique relationship to Jesus who promises them the kingdom because they have entrusted themselves to him and believed in his proclamation of the kingdom. Having described who his disciples are and what they can expect, Jesus is now ready to provide them with a teaching that will allow them to live as his disciples in the world. He will teach them how to live in a way that corresponds to the fullest meaning of God's law.

Living a More Abundant Righteousness 2

Jesus has chosen his disciples to be the salt of the earth and the light of the world. To focus their attention on the purpose of their discipleship, he has exhorted them to practice their good works for others to see so that others will praise their heavenly Father. But what are these good works and how should the disciples practice them? This is the question Jesus addresses in the central part of the sermon in which he teaches his disciples what it means to live in a way that perfectly accords with God's will (5:17–7:12).

The Law and the Prophets Fulfilled (5:17-20)

Jesus proclaims the Sermon on the Mount in his capacity as the messianic Son of God, the one who comes to fulfill the promises God made to Israel in the Law and the Prophets. Consequently, at the outset of the sermon, he dispels any notion that he has come to abolish the Law or the Prophets. The purpose of his teaching, he insists, is to fulfill rather than to abolish the Law and the Prophets. But what does Jesus mean when he says that he comes to fulfill the Law and the Prophets? Does he mean that he comes to do and observe them completely, to add what is missing, to bring out their inner meaning, to realize their prophetic goal?

47

These are some of the possible meanings of the verb "to fulfill." The manner in which Matthew employs this verb throughout his gospel, however, suggests that Jesus brings the Law and the Prophets to their prophetic fulfillment in himself through his ministry of preaching, teaching, and healing. For example, throughout the gospel, Matthew frequently employs "fulfillment quotations" to indicate that particular events in the life and ministry of Jesus are the fulfillment of what is written in Scripture (Matt 1:22; 2:17; 4:14; 8:17; 12:17; 13:35; 21:4; 26:56; 27:9). To give just one example, after Joseph is told that Mary has conceived through the power of the Holy Spirit, Matthew writes, "All this took place *to fulfill* what had been spoken by the Lord through the prophet: 'Look, the virgin shall conceive and bear a son, and they shall name him Emmanuel,' which means, 'God is with us' " (1:22-23). The use of "fulfill" in this and other fulfillment quotations suggests that it has a similar meaning here in Matt 5:17: Jesus' teaching will bring the Law and the Prophets to their prophetic fulfillment by disclosing their full meaning as intended by God.

To highlight the enduring validity of the Law, Jesus insists that not even the smallest letter of the Law, not even one of its diacritical marks, will disappear until heaven and earth pass away, until everything has been accomplished. The plain meaning of Jesus' words is that the Law will endure until everything is accomplished. But when will everything be accomplished: at Jesus' death and resurrection, at the end of the ages? If all things are accomplished at Jesus' death and resurrection, there is a sense in which the Law has come to its prophetic fulfillment as Paul affirms in Rom 10:4, where he writes that Christ is the end of the Law. But if all things will be accomplished at the end of the ages, then the Law endures until the end of the ages. Contemporary Christianity has, for all practical purposes, adopted a mediating solution. On the one hand, recognizing that Christ's death and resurrection is the climatic point of salvation history, Christians no longer observe the cultic and ritual prescriptions of the Law, which they see as fulfilled in Christ, as described in the Epistle to the Hebrews. On the other hand, recognizing that there is a final act to the drama of salvation that will not be completed until the Son of Man returns at the end of the ages, Christians continue to practice the moral demands of the Law as taught by Jesus the Messiah. The manner in which Jesus frames his teaching for his disciples, however, should be a reminder to contemporary disciples that the Messiah did not come to abolish the Law God gave to Israel at Sinai but to fulfill it by teaching its fullest meaning.

Aware that some commandments of the Law are more important than others and that his disciples might be tempted to observe the more important matters of the Law but not the less important ones—a temptation contemporary disciples still face—Jesus highlights the importance of observing *all* the commandments of the Law, the least as well as the greatest. Consequently, he warns disciples who would violate the *least* commandments and teach others to do the same that they will be *least* in the kingdom of heaven, whereas those who do them and teach others to do so will be called the greatest in the kingdom of heaven. At the outset of the sermon, then, Jesus insists that just as he observes and teaches the whole of God's Law, so his disciples must do the same. The observance of God's Law is not a matter of picking and choosing what is important but of doing and teaching *all* that God commands, even though certain prescriptions may seem strange and insignificant in the eyes of the disciples. In effect, Jesus adopts a maximalist rather than a minimalist approach to the Law.

Having forewarned his disciples that the teaching that follows will not abolish the Law and the Prophets, thereby maintaining continuity with God's plan of salvation, Jesus tells them that if their righteousness does not exceed that of the scribes and Pharisees they will not enter the kingdom of heaven (5:20). Although Jesus will criticize the way in which the scribes and Pharisees practice the Law (see Matthew 23), he readily acknowledges that they practice a certain righteousness. They observe the Law: they do not murder, they do not commit adultery, they do not swear falsely, and so on. But Jesus' disciples are to practice a more abundant righteousness that exceeds and surpasses the legal observance of the scribes and Pharisees. Exactly what Jesus means by this will be apparent only after we have heard the entire sermon. By way of anticipation, however, we can say that the more abundant righteousness Jesus teaches is rooted in an observance of the Law that expresses the fullness of God's will. It is a righteousness that originates in the heart, seeking to do the Law in a way that accords with God's will. It is a righteousness that accords with the inner demands of the Law of which Jeremiah spoke (Jer 31:31-34) as well as its legal requirements as described in the Decalogue. At the outset of his great teaching on righteousness, then, Jesus promises something new as well as continuity. On the one hand, the teaching that follows will not violate or abolish the Law. On the other, Jesus will introduce something new by bringing the Law to its prophetic fulfillment; he will reveal the full meaning of God's commandment.

The Six Antitheses (5:21-48)

The six statements that follow are traditionally called "antitheses" since Jesus juxtaposes what he says to his disciples with what was said to those of ancient times. The use of this term, however, can be misleading since it could imply that Jesus' teaching stands in opposition to the Law, thereby contradicting what he has just said about fulfilling the Law and the Prophets. Before turning to these statements, then, it will be helpful to say something about the form, structure, and christological significance of these antitheses.

First, the antitheses share a similar form. Each begins with a statement of what was said to Israel of old when God gave the Law. Next, Jesus presents his teaching in a way that stands in sharp contrast to what was said to those of ancient times. For example, in the first antithesis Jesus begins, "*You have heard that it was said to those of ancient times,* 'You shall not murder'; and 'whoever murders shall be liable to judgment.'" Next, he says, "*But I say to you* that if you are angry with a brother or sister, you will be liable to judgment; and if you insult a brother or sister, you will be liable to the council; and if you say, 'You fool,' you will be liable to the hell of fire." This juxtaposition between what was said to the wilderness generation and what Jesus says to his disciples accounts for the use of "antitheses" to describe this part of the sermon.

Second, although the six antitheses have a similar structure, there is a slight variation in their formulation. Whereas the first and fourth use long opening formulas, the remaining antitheses employ shorter opening formulas. And whereas in the first three antitheses, Jesus says *whoever* does such and such, in the last three he begins with a negative imperative, *do not.* Thus the antitheses are structured as two groups of three (just as the first eight beatitudes are structured as two groups of four), the second group beginning with the adverb "again" and the longer opening formula of the first antithesis.

> *You have heard that it was said to those of ancient times.* . . .
>> But I say to you, *whoever.* . . .
> You have heard that it was said. . . .
>> But I say to you, *whoever.* . . .
> It was also said. . . .
>> But I say to you, *whoever.* . . .
>
> **Again**, *you have heard that it was said to those of ancient times.* . . .
>> But I say to you, *do not.* . . .
> You have heard that it was said. . . .
>> But I say to you, *do not.* . . .
> You have heard that it was said. . . .
>> But I say to you, *do not.* . . .

Third, the most startling aspect of these statements is the christological implication of the juxtaposition they establish between what was said and what Jesus says. Whereas it was God who spoke to the wilderness generation, it is Jesus who speaks to his disciples. To grasp the impact of this juxtaposition, it is important to remember that Jesus speaks in this way because he is the messianic Son of God. He does not come as another rabbi who provides his interpretation of the Law. He does not come as a new

Moses. He comes as the Son of God who reveals the prophetic meaning of God's Law to his disciples. In doing so, he does not oppose his teaching to the teaching God gave to the wilderness generation as if he were correcting or supplanting God's Torah. Rather, he comes as the Spirit-endowed Son of God who speaks with the authority of his Father. God spoke to the wilderness generation, and the Son speaks to his disciples in a way that reveals the prophetic meaning of God's words—a fuller teaching of the Law, which the wilderness generation could not understand because of its hardness of heart.

***Not even anger* (5:21-26)**. The first antithesis begins by citing the commandment of the Decalogue, "You shall not murder" (Exod 20:13; Deut 5:17), which Jesus supplements with a statement that points to the penalty for murder, "Whoever murders shall be liable to judgment" (Exod 21:12, Lev 24:17). But whereas the Decalogue speaks of murder, Jesus warns his disciples that the one who is angry will be liable to judgment, the one who insults another will be brought before the council for punishment, and the one who calls another a fool will be liable to the fire of Gehenna. The punishments for the infractions Jesus envisions grow in intensity (from judgment before a local court, to judgment before the high council, to eternal judgment) and appear disproportionate to the offense. Does Jesus mean that disciples are never to become angry? Didn't he become angry when he cleansed the temple? Is it so serious an offense to insult another or call someone a fool? Didn't Paul insult his opponents and call the Galatians foolish (Gal 3:1)? Doesn't Jesus call the scribes and the Pharisees blind fools (Matt 23:17)?

Before responding to these questions it will be helpful to listen to the rest of the antitheses. Having warned his disciples to control their temper, Jesus provides them with two examples, one related to worship and the other to everyday life. First, reconciliation with enemies is more important than worship. Consequently, if a disciple is bringing a gift to the altar and remembers that his brother has something against him, he is to take the initiative and be reconciled to his brother before offering the gift. Second, if an opponent is bringing a disciple to court, the disciple is to come to terms with the opponent as quickly as possible lest he be handed over to the judge and put in prison. As in the first case, it is the disciples who are to take the initiative and be reconciled with those who are estranged from them.

The demands of these two examples are extreme. After all, is a person really to leave the gift at the altar and be reconciled with someone who may be in another city or country? Must disciples be reconciled with enemies who accuse them falsely? Taken at face value, Jesus' teaching seems exaggerated and impractical. Since this is an issue we will encounter again, it is best to confront it now. If we do not, Jesus' teaching will be interpreted as a new set of rules and regulations, and the sermon will become the occasion for a new casuistry. But Jesus does not come to bring a new set of rules and laws; he comes to fulfill the Law and the Prophets. In this instance, he fulfills the Law by identifying the root cause of murder: murder begins with anger, with the insulting word, with a slur. Consequently, whereas the Law forbids murder, Jesus calls upon his disciples to avoid those things that lead to murder. Whereas the Law forbids the act of murder, Jesus forbids the angry word that leads to murder. The commandment not to murder remains unchanged, but Jesus now reveals its meaning as intended by God. The full meaning of the commandment is to avoid the angry insult that results in murder. Practically speaking there will be moments when people will become angry, sometimes for a righteous cause, other times needlessly. And there will be times when people will hurl insults and slurs at each other. But in all of these instances Jesus' disciples must remember that anger and insult have the potential of escalating to a point that disciples lose control of their inner self. At such moments anger can lead to murder. Thus the prophetic meaning of the Law is to avoid even anger.

Not even the lustful look (5:27-30). The second antithesis is similar to the first. Like the first, it quotes from the Decalogue. Citing the sixth commandment (Exod 20:14; Deut 5:18), Jesus reminds his disciples what God said: "You shall not commit adultery." Next, he brings the Decalogue to its prophetic fulfillment by saying, "But I say to you that everyone who looks on a woman with lust has already committed adultery with her in his heart." This is a startling statement in a world accustomed to thinking of the woman rather than the man as the one who commits adultery. Whereas the ancient world put the onus for marital faithfulness on the woman, who was viewed as the property of her husband, Jesus puts it on the man. As in the first antithesis, he goes beyond the plain meaning of the commandment that forbids the physical act of adultery in order to reveal its prophetic meaning: just as murder begins with anger, so adultery begins with the lustful look, the desire that no longer respects the woman as a personal subject but turns her into an object of lust. The whole purpose of the commandment, says Jesus, is not merely to prevent the physical act of adultery but to ensure that men and women will treat each other as persons worthy of honor and respect rather than as objects of pleasure. The lustful desire may not be the physical act of adultery, but it is adultery inasmuch as the consent has already been given for the act of adultery. For even if the man never finds the opportunity to commit the adultery he desires, he has already resolved to do what the commandment forbids. Consequently, whereas righteousness requires people to refrain from the physical act of adultery, the more abundant righteousness requires them to refrain from the lustful desire, which is the essence of adultery.

As in the first antithesis, Jesus provides his disciples with examples of what they should do to insure they will practice a more abundant righteousness. The examples he gives are extreme, and most readers will understand that he is employing hyperbole to make his point—although some have mistakenly taken these words literally. If your right eye causes you to sin, tear it out. If your right hand causes you to sin, cut it off. Better to lose part of your body, even the most precious part, than to be thrown into the fiery pit of Gehenna. The two parts of the body Jesus chooses for his examples are especially appropriate since desire begins with sight and touch. The eye will continue to play an important role, albeit in different ways, in the rest of the sermon (Matt 5:38; 6:22-23; 7:3). But here, the eye and the hand are best taken as occasions for sin. When such occasions arise, it is better for disciples to avoid them entirely than to suppose they can overcome them.

The similarity between the first two antitheses provides an insight into the prophetic dimension of the Law and the Prophets that Jesus reveals. The Law forbids murder and adultery, but the prophetic meaning of the Law goes beyond avoiding these acts. It requires disciples to avoid what leads to them: the angry word, the lustful look.

Faithfulness to one's spouse (5:31-32). Jesus begins his third antithesis with the shortest of all the opening formulas: "It was also said." Instead of quoting from the Decalogue, however, he quotes from a text of Deuteronomy that explains the procedure for divorce in ancient Israel. To understand the text, it will be helpful to read it within its context.

> Suppose a man enters into marriage with a woman, but she does not please him because he finds *something objectionable about her*, and *so he writes her a certificate of divorce*, puts it in her hand, and sends her out of his house; she then leaves his house and goes off to become another man's wife. Then suppose the second man dislikes her, writes her a bill of divorce, puts it in her hand, and sends her out of his house (or the second man who married her dies); her first husband, who sent her away, is not permitted to take her again to be his wife after she has been defiled; for that would be abhorrent to the LORD, and you shall not bring guilt on the land that the LORD your God is giving you as a possession. (Deut 24:1-4)

There are several things to note here. First, this text indicates the procedure for divorce; it does not command divorce. When a husband divorces his wife, he must give her a written bill of dismissal that indicates that he has divorced her and that she is free to marry another. Second, while a husband had the right to divorce his wife in ancient Israel, a wife did not have the right to divorce her husband. Put simply, divorce was for the benefit of the man and not for the benefit of the woman. Third, in this case from Deuteronomy, this issue involves more than the procedure for divorce; it concerns what a man can and cannot do if his divorced wife marries another man. Should she marry another, the first husband cannot take her back because she has been defiled; and if he takes her back, even if the second husband dies, this will defile the land of Israel. Later, in a controversy with the Pharisees, Jesus will explain that Moses allowed the men of Israel to divorce their wives because they were hard-hearted, but it was not so from the beginning. And because they were hard of heart, they did not understand that divorce was not God's original intention for man and woman (Matt 19:1-12).

Having quoted this text, which describes the procedure for divorce in ancient Israel, Jesus provides his disciples with a teaching that reveals the original will of God: a man who divorces his wife causes her to commit adultery because she is still his wife in the eyes of God. Likewise, if a man marries a divorced woman, he commits adultery because the woman is still married to her husband. Jesus does, however, provide for one exception—except for *porneia*—a Greek word that points to gross immorality, usually of a sexual nature. In providing this exception, Jesus enters into one of the legal debates of his day: What did Moses mean in Deuteronomy 24 when he spoke of *something objectionable about her*? Can a man divorce his wife because she displeased him in some small matter? Or is divorce reserved for something more serious? While some took a lenient approach to this debate and would have allowed divorce for insignificant reasons, Jesus sides with those who adopted a rigorist approach. Divorce does not correspond with God's original will for man and woman who become one flesh when they are joined in matrimony; for divorce separates what God has joined together (Matt 19:4-6). If there is to be an exception, it can only be for the gravest of reasons.

The exception clause is unique to Matthew's Gospel. When Jesus speaks about divorce in the Gospels of Mark and Luke (Mark 10:11-12; Luke 16:18), there is no exception whatsoever. Likewise, when Paul recalls the teaching of Jesus about divorce, there is no exception (1 Cor 7:10-11). This raises the question of the origin of the exception clause in Matthew's gospel. Does it come from Jesus, or does it come from a time when it became necessary to deal with troublesome marital issues in this church? Whatever the answer to this difficult historical question, the meaning and significance of this text is clear. Jesus reveals the prophetic meaning of God's Law by teaching his disciples that husbands who divorce their wives commit adultery, and men who marry divorced women do the same. If there is an exception, it is for only the most serious cases of immorality, cases that are not the norm but tragic exceptions. Whereas Roman Catholicism tends to follow the teaching of Jesus as witnessed by Mark, Luke, and Paul, Protestant and Orthodox churches have found in the text of Matthew a way to deal with serious pastoral issues. Like the antithesis on adultery, however, the purpose of Jesus' teaching on divorce is to reveal the prophetic meaning of the Law to his disciples, which in both instances seeks to protect the dignity of man and woman.

Telling the truth at all times (5:33-37). With the fourth antithesis Jesus returns to the longer introductory formula he used in the first antithesis. This longer formula plus the use of the adverb "again" signals that he is beginning a new series of three antitheses, many of which will deal with laws found in the Book of Leviticus. Accordingly, Jesus begins by reminding his disciples what was said to the ancient generation. In doing so, he provides them with a quotation that brings parts of two texts together, one from Lev 19:12 ("And *you shall not swear falsely* by my name, profaning the name of your God: I am the LORD"), the other from Num 30:2 ("*When a man makes a vow to the LORD, or swears an oath* to bind himself by a pledge, he shall not break his word; *he shall do according to all that proceeds out of his mouth*"). Employing a strong negative imperative, Jesus then instructs his disciples not to swear at all. They are not to swear by heaven because it is God's throne, nor are they to swear by the earth because it is God's footstool: "Heaven is my throne and the earth is my footstool; what is the house that you would build for me, and what is my resting place?"

(Isa 66:1). They are not to swear by the city of Jerusalem because it is the city of the Great King, God: "Mount Zion, in the far north, the city of the great King" (Ps 48:2). Nor are they to swear by their own head since they do not have the power to make a single hair white or black. The point of Jesus' examples is that those who swear by heaven, by earth, or by Jerusalem presume to call upon God as their witness, while those who swear by their own head invoke themselves as witnesses even though they are powerless to alter the most insignificant aspects of their lives.

Having instructed his disciples what they should *not* do, Jesus employs a positive imperative to instruct them what to do: When they mean "yes" they should say "yes," and when they mean "no" they should say "no." Jesus' disciples should be people of such perfect integrity that there is no need for them to take an oath to assure others they are telling the truth. The problem with oaths is that they presume to call upon God as a witness and imply that people are bound to tell the truth only when they are under oath. Jesus brings the Law to its prophetic fulfillment by pointing to the full meaning of God's will as revealed in those laws pertaining to oaths. The purpose of swearing an oath is to insure honesty and the fulfillment of promises. But if this is the purpose of an oath, then, there is no need for Jesus' disciples, who ought to be people of perfect integrity, to swear such oaths. When they say "yes" they mean "yes," and when they say "no" they mean "no." Anything more is superfluous; it comes from "the evil one."

Jesus' teaching on oaths and his condemnation of the way in which the scribes and Pharisees take oaths provides a good example of what he means by the greater righteousness. Jesus does not criticize the Pharisees and scribes for taking oaths since the Law provides for them. But he does criticize the casuistic manner in which they take oaths. Distinguishing between the temple and the gold of the temple, and between the altar and the gift on the altar, the Pharisees and scribes maintain that a person is not bound by an oath sworn by the temple or by an oath sworn by the altar of the temple, but one is bound by an oath sworn by the gold of the temple or the gift on the altar of the temple. In face of such casuistry, Jesus points out that it is the altar that makes the gift holy, and if one swears by the temple then one swears by God who dwells in the temple (Matt 23:16-22). In speaking to his own disciples, however, Jesus forbids all oaths because the original purpose of oaths is to ensure an honesty and integrity that ought to be the hallmark of discipleship. Thus, whereas the righteousness of the Pharisees and scribes is a righteousness based on fulfilling their oaths, the more abundant righteousness of Jesus' disciples is a righteousness based on their perfect integrity and honesty that no longer requires them to take oaths to assure others of their honesty.

Although Jesus' teaching on oaths finds a strong echo in the letter of James ("Above all, my beloved, do not swear, either by heaven or by earth or by any other oath, but let your 'Yes' be yes and your 'No' be no, so that you may not fall under condemnation" [Jas 5:12]), there are a number of texts in the New Testament that present oath-taking in a more positive light. For example, Paul often affirms the veracity of what he says by calling on God as his witness (Rom 1:9; 2 Cor 1:23; Gal 1:20; Phil 1:8). In the Letter to the Hebrews, God guarantees the veracity of what he speaks by an oath (Heb 6:16-17), confirming the high priesthood of Christ through an oath (Heb 7:20-21, 28). And of course most Christians take oaths in civil settings today. So what are we to make of Jesus' teaching that his disciples are not to swear oaths at all?

If one approaches the Sermon on the Mount merely as a new set of rules and regulations, it is difficult to understand how one could take any oath today. But Jesus is not establishing a new set of rules and regulations. He is revealing God's original will by bringing the Law and the Prophets to their prophetic fulfillment. Accordingly, just as the fuller meaning of the commandment not to commit murder includes avoiding anger, so the fuller meaning of the laws concerning oaths is perfect honesty and integrity. Just as those who refrain from anger will avoid murder, so those who are perfectly honest have no need to take oaths. This is why there is no place within the community of Jesus' disciples for oaths. But inasmuch as his disciples live in a world where people are not always honest and transparent, there will be times that disciples will be called upon by the wider society to take oaths to insure an honesty that Jesus' disciples should always maintain, even when they are not under oath.

Overcoming evil through love (5:38-42). The fifth antithesis, like the second, begins with a shorter introductory formula followed by a quotation from the Mosaic Law found in Exod 21:24 and Lev 24:20: "You have heard that it was said, 'An eye for an eye and a tooth for a tooth.'" Employing a negative imperative, Jesus juxtaposes his teaching with this prescription of the Law: "But I say to you, do not resist an evildoer." To illustrate what he means, Jesus provides his disciples with four examples. If someone strikes them on the right cheek, they should offer the left as well. If someone sues them for their long inner garment (the tunic worn close to the skin), they are to give that person the outer garment as well. If someone presses them into service and requires them to carry their baggage one mile, they should go two miles. And if someone wants to borrow from them, they are not to refuse. In a word, whereas the Mosaic Law allowed a limited and proportionate retaliation, Jesus instructs his disciples to forego what the Law allows, thereby practicing a more abundant righteousness.

On first hearing, the law of retaliation that Jesus quotes from Exodus and Leviticus seems harsh and cruel. Its purpose, however, was to mitigate rather than to encourage violence. Thus if a person harms another, the injured party can require "life for life, eye for eye, tooth for tooth, hand for hand, foot for foot, burn for burn, wound for wound, stripe for stripe" (Exod 21:23-25), but no more. In calling upon his disciples to forego all retaliation Jesus reveals the deeper meaning of the Law, which sought to restrain violence by allowing only a proportionate response. The more abundant righteousness that Jesus teaches, then, reflects the deepest meaning of the Law inasmuch as it goes beyond the mitigation of violence by forsaking all violence.

The four examples Jesus provides presuppose situations of hostility: an evil person strikes a disciple, brings him to court, forces him into service, or makes an unreasonable request to borrow something. In every instance a reasonable person would say that the disciple should resist. Jesus' teaching, however, has something else in view. It begins with the premise that resisting evil does not overcome evil. To the contrary, resistance gives evil its power and force. But when evil encounters sheer goodness rather than resistance, it loses its power and force. This is why Paul writes, "Do not be overcome by evil, *but overcome evil with good*" (Rom 12:21), and again, "See that none of you repays evil for evil, but always seek to do good to one another and to all" (1 Thess 5:15).

Ancient Israel was not unaware of the futility of repaying evil with evil. Confident of God's vindication, the Book of Proverbs counsels, "Do not say, 'I will repay evil'; wait for the LORD, and he will help you" (Prov 20:22). Aware that evil will eventually come to the end it deserves, Proverbs adds, "Do not say, 'I will do to others as they have done to me; I will pay them back for what they have done'" (Prov 24:29). Jesus, however, gives this teaching its full meaning by the example of his life: "When he was abused, he did not return abuse; when he suffered, he did not threaten; but he entrusted himself to the one who judges justly" (1 Pet 2:23).

But how are disciples to put this teaching into practice? Is such teaching practical? Can it be carried out in everyday life? What is one to do in the face of extreme evil such as appeared in Nazi Germany? Once more, it would be a mistake to turn Jesus' teaching into a set of rules and laws. As in the other antitheses, he fulfills the Law by revealing God's will. Understood in this light, it should be clear that evil cannot overcome evil—only good can overcome evil. Those who hear the sermon with the ears of disciples understand this and witness to the world what seems foolish and utterly impractical; they refuse to resist evil with evil. Such an ethic, however, is possible only in a community of like-minded disciples committed to non-violence, a community dedicated to overcoming evil with goodness. While it is difficult to practice such an ethic in a world infected by Adam's sin, it is not impossible for Jesus' disciples. To the contrary, this is precisely the witness the community of Jesus' disciples must bring to the world, a witness that mirrors the example of its Lord who overcame the power of sin through the weakness and folly of the cross.

Loving even the enemy (5:43-48). Jesus' sixth and final antithesis is the climax of his teaching and distinguishes him from his contemporaries. Whereas it was said, "You shall love your neighbor and hate your enemy," Jesus instructs his disciples to love their enemies and pray for those who persecute them so that they will be sons and daughters of their heavenly Father who does not discriminate between the righteous and the unrighteous in the realm of nature where the sun shines and the rain falls on both. In support of his teaching, Jesus asks his disciples two rhetorical questions that explain why they must go beyond the law of reciprocity. First, if they only love those who love them, how will their behavior differ from that of the tax collectors who do the same? Second, if they only greet each other, how will their behavior differ from that of the Gentiles who do the same? The more abundant righteousness the disciples are to practice requires them to go beyond the law of reciprocity that only requires them to do good to those who do good to them. Jesus' disciples are to love even their enemies. Thus the sixth antithesis is similar to the fifth in that it requires disciples to treat those who mistreat them in a wholly new way: instead of retaliating they are not to resist the evil person, and instead of hating the enemy they are to love those who hate them and pray for those who persecute them.

The portion of the Law that Jesus quotes here comes from the Holiness Code (Leviticus 17–26). But whereas Lev 19:18 reads, "You shall not take vengeance or bear a grudge against any of your people, but *you shall love your neighbor as yourself.* I am the LORD," Jesus quotes the Law as saying, "You shall love your neighbor *and hate your enemy.*" Thus Jesus includes a phrase that is not found in the text of Leviticus or in the rest of the Old Testament. Furthermore, although his teaching is distinctive, it is not unknown to the Old Testament. For example, in the Book of the Covenant (Exod 20:23–23:19), Israel is instructed, "When you come upon your enemy's ox or donkey going astray, you shall bring it back. When you see the donkey of one who hates you lying under its burden and you would hold back from setting it free, you must help to set it free" (Exod 23:4-5). Likewise, the Book of Proverbs cautions those seeking wisdom not to rejoice when their enemies fall or stumble, lest the LORD be displeased (Prov 24:17-18), and it advises the wise to give bread to their enemies when they are hungry and water when they are thirsty, for by doing so they will "heap coals of fire" on the heads of their enemies, and the LORD will reward them (Prov 25:21-22). But alongside of this teaching that points to the advantage of doing what is good to one's enemy, there was another tradition that spoke of hatred for Israel's enemies. For example, the psalmist writes, "Do I not hate those who hate you, O LORD? And do I not loathe those who rise up against you? I hate them with perfect hatred; I count them my enemies" (Ps 139:21-22).

By adding the words "and hate your enemies," then, Jesus indicates how the commandment to love one's neighbor was to be practiced in everyday life. In most instances, it was restricted to fellow Israelites and those foreigners who resided in the land of Israel (Lev 19:34). This is why the lawyer asks Jesus, "And who is my neighbor?" (Luke 10:29). The lawyer wants to know Jesus' opinion on a disputed question: Is my neighbor my fellow Israelite, as most would have maintained? Or, do non-Israelites fall into the category of neighbor as well? In response, Jesus tells the parable of the Good Samaritan, which exhorts the lawyer to be a neighbor to anyone in need, thereby redefining the neighbor as anyone in need. The addition of the words "and hate your enemies," then, indicates the way in which the commandment of Lev 19:18 was understood by many of Jesus' contemporaries.

By teaching his disciples to love their enemies as well as their neighbors, Jesus reveals the deeper meaning of the Law, and he challenges his disciples to practice a more abundant righteousness. Whereas the righteousness of many of Jesus' contemporaries was expressed in love for one's fellow Israelite and hatred for Israel's enemies, the more abundant righteousness transcends national and ethnic boundaries to include those who are categorized as enemies because of their national or ethnic background (an understanding of enemy that contemporary culture has still to overcome). Furthermore, by requiring his disciples to pray for those who persecute them, Jesus reminds them of what he said in the eighth and ninth beatitudes: they will be persecuted on account of him for their righteousness. When that day comes, they are to transcend the righteous behavior of their contemporaries by praying for their enemies.

Jesus' teaching on love for one's enemy has had a profound and lasting influence on his followers, even though they have not always been faithful to it. When he was being stoned to death, Stephen cried out, "Lord, do not hold this sin against them" (Act 7:60), a phrase that recalls Jesus' words, "Father, forgive them; for they do not know what they are doing" (Luke 23:34). Paul echoes Jesus' teaching when he writes, "Bless those who persecute you; bless and do not curse them" (Rom 12:14), and again, "See that none of you repays evil for evil, but always seeks to do good to one another and to all" (1 Thess 5:15). Peter makes a similar exhortation when he writes, "Do not repay evil for evil or abuse for abuse; but, on the contrary, repay with a blessing. It is for this that you were called—that you might inherit a blessing" (1 Pet 3:9).

Jesus concludes this antithesis with a statement that provides a profound reason for the disciples to love their enemies: "Be perfect, therefore, as your heavenly Father is perfect" (Matt 5:48). By loving their enemies, the disciples will imitate their heavenly Father who does not withhold the sun or the rain from the unrighteous. In being perfect they will show that they are sons and daughters of God, disciples of the Son of God. But what does it mean to be "perfect," and how can one be perfect as God is perfect?

If one conceives of being perfect in terms of perfection, it is impossible for human beings to be perfect. Human beings are imperfect and will always make mistakes. But that is not the meaning of "perfect" (*teleios*) here. While the word has different shades of meaning in the New Testament ("mature," "initiated," "fully developed"), its sense here is to be whole, entire, undivided in allegiance and devotion to God. Therefore, those who are perfect are those completely devoted to God; they are people who are whole and entire in their allegiance to God just as God is whole, entire, and undivided. This concept is found several times in the

Old Testament. For example, Moses tells the Israelites, "You must remain *completely loyal* to the LORD your God" (Deut 18:13); and when Solomon brings the ark of the covenant to the temple, he stands before the assembly of Israel and tells the people that their heart must be *"wholly devoted* to the LORD, our God, observing his statues and keeping his commandments, as on this day" (1 Kgs 8:61). The same word occurs in the account of the rich young man who asks Jesus what good deed he must do to gain eternal life (Matt 19:16). Jesus tells him to keep the commandments, and the man replies that he has. Jesus then says, "If you wish to be *perfect*, go, sell your possessions, and give the money to the poor, and you will have treasure in heaven; then come, follow me" (Matt 19:21). It is at this point that the man leaves grieving because he has many possessions. He cannot be perfect because his heart is divided between his desire for eternal life and his desire for possessions. In counseling the man to sell his possessions and follow him, Jesus invites him to be whole, complete, and undivided in his devotion to God. Disciples will be perfect as their heavenly Father is perfect, then, if they love even their enemies. For just as God does not discriminate in his love for humanity, neither should disciples discriminate in their love for others.

Jesus introduced the concept of wholehearted devotion to God in the sixth beatitude when he spoke of the pure of heart. In the next section of the sermon he will instruct his disciples to be undivided in their allegiance to God by refusing to practice their piety in the way the hypocrites do who seek the praise of humans as well as the praise of God. Before turning to this teaching, however, it will be helpful to make some concluding remarks about the six antitheses.

First, although Jesus has framed his teaching in a series of antitheses, he fulfills rather than abolishes the Law by revealing its deepest meaning. Such a revelation is necessary to overcome the hardness of heart that prevents human beings from understanding the full meaning of God's will as revealed in the Law.

Second, the greater righteousness Jesus teaches requires disciples to do more than the Law requires and, at times, to forego what the Law allows. And so Jesus requires his disciples to avoid anger and lust as well as murder and adultery. He requires them to be faithful to their spouses and to tell the truth at all times, even when they are not under oath. He requires them to forego vengeance and to love their enemies.

Third, if the disciples have understood Jesus' teaching in these antitheses, there is no need for him to comment on the entire Law. What they have learned from this teaching will enable them to interpret the rest of the Law in a similar way. Thus the antitheses provide disciples with a way to understand the deeper requirements of the whole of God's Law.

Piety without Hypocrisy 3

In his first instruction on righteousness, Jesus juxtaposed what was spoken to the wilderness generation ("You have heard that it was said") with his own teaching ("But I say to you"). His purpose in doing this was to reveal the full intent of what God spoke to that generation rather than to abolish the Law or the Prophets. Consequently, the commandments of the Decalogue remain in force, but Jesus' disciples are to fulfill their deepest intent. The Law made provision for divorce, for the taking of oaths, and for retaliation, but Jesus tells his disciples to practice a more abundant righteousness that foregoes these provisions of the Law for the sake of a greater righteousness. Finally, he brings the commandment to love one's neighbor to its fulfillment by including within its purview the enemy as well as those who belong to the people of Israel. Rather than provide a new interpretation of the Law, then, Jesus fulfills it by revealing its full meaning and intention. Understood in this way, his teaching is the full revelation of the Law.

In his second teaching on righteousness (6:1-18), Jesus considers three works of Jewish piety whereby people manifest their righteousness: almsgiving, prayer, and fasting. Practiced correctly, these acts of piety show that those who do them are in a right relationship with God, and so they can be called righteous. But just as it is possible to do the prescriptions of the Law in a formal way that does not produce a more abundant righteousness, so it is possible to practice these works of piety without standing in a right relationship to God. This is why Jesus contrasts the way in which the "hypocrites" practice these works of righteousness with the way in which his disciples should practice them.

Although Jesus frequently calls the scribes and the Pharisees hypocrites (see Matt 23:13,15, 23, 25, 27, 29), he does not mention them in this section, which suggests that the designation "hypocrite" is not intended exclusively for the scribes and Pharisees; it includes all who are not perfectly whole and undivided in their allegiance to God. The Greek word that underlies "hypocrite" here refers to an actor who plays a role on a stage, pretending to be someone else. This, of course, is precisely what good actors do: they make their audience believe they are someone else. On the basis of this theatrical usage, the word eventually took on a negative meaning in reference to people who pretend to be what they are not. Hypocrites, then, are duplicitous because they pretend to be someone else. While this is what an actor is supposed to do, it is not what people are called to do in everyday life where their exterior comportment should correspond to their interior self. Like Jesus' six antitheses, his teaching on almsgiving, prayer, and fasting manifests a clearly defined structure that can be outlined in this way.

Jesus' Introductory Admonition (6:1)
    Warning (6:1a)
    Consequence (6:1b)
Jesus' Teaching on Alms (6:2-4)
    The negative example of the hypocrites (6:2a)
    A reward statement (6:2b)
    The positive conduct Jesus requires (6:3-4a)
    A reward statement (6:4b)
Jesus' Teaching on Prayer (6:5-15)
    The negative example of the hypocrites (6:5a)
    A reward statement (6:5b)

The positive conduct Jesus requires (6:6a)
A reward statement (6:6b)
Introduction to the Lord's Prayer (6:7-8)
The Lord's Prayer (6:9-13)
Conclusion to the Lord's Prayer (6:14-15)
Jesus' Teaching on Fasting (6:16-18)
The negative example of the hypocrites (6:16a)
A reward statement (6:16b)
The positive conduct Jesus requires (16:17-18a)
A reward statement (16:18b)

There are two points to note here. The first is that after his introductory admonition to his disciples not to practice their righteousness in order to be seen by others, Jesus provides them with examples of what he means. Each example follows a similar pattern: (1) Jesus describes the behavior of those whom he calls "the hypocrites;" (2) He introduces a reward statement in which he says that the hypocrites have already received their reward in full; (3) He describes how his disciples should practice their piety; (4) He promises his disciples that their heavenly Father will reward them. There is, then, a certain similarity between these three examples and the six antitheses inasmuch as Jesus establishes a second set of contrasts. But whereas the contrast in the antitheses is between what was spoken and what Jesus says, here it is between piety done for public display and piety done for its own sake because it is the right thing to do.

The second point is the manner in which Jesus breaks this threefold pattern by introducing the Lord's Prayer between his teaching on prayer and fasting. Jesus' prayer becomes an expansion of his teaching on how to pray. But how is his prayer related to the rest of the sermon, and why does he introduce it at this point, the midpoint of the sermon? To answer these questions, we must pay attention to the relationship between Jesus' prayer, his sermon, and his teaching on righteousness.

The Danger of Hypocrisy (6:1)

Just as Jesus prefaces the six antitheses with a statement that provides his disciples with an initial understanding of what he is about to say (5:17-20), so he prefaces his teaching on almsgiving, prayer, and fasting with a similar, albeit, briefer, statement: his disciples are not to practice their righteousness in order to be seen and praised by others. With this statement Jesus identifies a central challenge of the religious life: how to practice righteousness with an undivided heart. He warns his disciples not to practice their righteousness (NRSV, "piety") for the purpose of gaining the praise of others. For if they do, they will not receive a reward from their Father in heaven. They are to practice their righteousness in secret, for its own sake, because it is the right thing to do.

At the beginning of the sermon, after the beatitudes, Jesus said, "let your light shine before others, so that they may see your good works and give glory to your Father in heaven" (5:16), but here he instructs them to beware of practicing their righteousness in order to be seen by others. So which is it? Are disciples to do everything in secret so that only God will see, or are they to let their good works shine forth so that others will praise their heavenly Father? The fact that Jesus makes both statements within the same sermon suggests that he is approaching the question of good deeds or acts of righteousness from two perspectives. At the beginning of the sermon, he tells the disciples that they are the light of the world and the salt of the earth because the message they bring is essential for the life of the world. Consequently, it is important for them to do good deeds in a way that the world will praise God rather than them. The purpose of displaying righteousness to the world, then, is to confirm the message of the kingdom and glorify their heavenly Father. But here Jesus approaches the topic of doing good deeds from another vantage point. First, while the disciples are to let the world see their good deeds, not every act of righteousness needs to be displayed before the world. Some acts should be done in a way known only to God, lest they become an occasion for others to praise the disciples rather than God.

Second, the purpose of every act of piety, whether done publicly or privately, is to praise God. Consequently, any act of righteousness that brings praise to oneself rather than to God is not a manifestation of the more abundant righteousness.

The distinction between what Jesus says at the beginning of the sermon and what he teaches here can be summarized in this way. While disciples can and must do their good deeds for others to see so that they will praise God, they are not to do their righteousness so that others will praise them. A decision about when and how to carry this out requires wisdom on the part of the disciples, just as it required wisdom on the part of Jesus who fasted in the wilderness and prayed in deserted places where no one could see him, but regularly performed his mighty works in a way that others would praise his heavenly Father.

Giving in Secret (6:2-4)

In the Old Testament, the Books of Tobit and Sirach speak extensively of almsgiving—acts of charity, usually in the form of monetary gifts, to those in need. Tobit is an outstanding example of one who performed many acts of charity for his kindred (Tob 1:3, 16). While prayer and fasting are good, the Book of Tobit teaches almsgiving with righteousness is better than both, and that it is better to give alms than to lay up gold (Tob 12:8). Almsgiving saves a person from death and purges away every sin (Tob 12:9). It is an excellent offering in the presence of the Most High (Tob 4:11). The Book of Sirach gives a similar assessment of almsgiving. It exhorts readers not to neglect giving alms (Sir 7:10) since almsgiving atones for sin and endures forever (Sir 3:30; 40:17). In the Gospel of Luke, Jesus tells the Pharisees, who are concerned with ritual purity, that if they want to be clean in God's sight they should give alms and everything will be made clean for them (Luke 11:41). He then exhorts his disciples to sell their possessions and give alms so that they will have unfailing treasure in heaven (Luke 12:33). Given the importance of almsgiving, it is not surprising that it is the first of Jesus' examples since prayer and fasting without concrete acts of charity are of little value. Jesus, however, is aware that even acts of almsgiving can be perverted if they are not done with a pure intention rooted in single-minded service to God. Consequently, he contrasts the way in which "the hypocrites" give alms with the manner in which his disciples are to give alms. Jesus' statement has four parts. First, he begins with the negative example of the hypocrites who sound the trumpet before them in the synagogue and streets so that others will know they are about to give alms. While it is possible that Jesus is referring to the way some actually broadcasted that they were about to give alms, it is more likely that he is employing hyperbole to make his point. By announcing what they are about to do, the hypocrites reveal that they are not whole and entire in their devotion to God since they are seeking the praise of humans beings as well as of God. Second, Jesus employs a short reward statement that he will repeat in the next two examples as well: "Truly I tell you, they have received their reward." Their reward is nothing less and nothing more than the praise and affirmation they seek from human beings. Having been praised for their almsgiving—which remains an act of righteousness—they have been paid in full; there will be no more reward. Third, Jesus instructs his disciples to give their alms in secret in a way that not even their left hand knows what the right hand (which is giving alms) is doing. Once more Jesus employs hyperbole to make his point; for if it is important that the left hand not know that the right hand has just given alms, then it is all the more important that no one, apart from God, knows that the disciple has given alms. Fourth, Jesus concludes with a second reward statement that he will repeat in the following two examples: "and your Father who sees in secret will reward you." As in the beatitudes, the reward that Jesus promises is eschatological in nature: the praise and approval of God that will come with the kingdom and endure forever.

The contrast that Jesus establishes in this first example, and that he will repeat in the next two, is a contrast between the hypocrites and those who are perfect so that what Jesus says here functions as a commentary on his injunction that disciples are to be perfect as their heavenly Father is perfect. Whereas the hypocrite is a person of divided loyalty—seeking to please humans as well as God—the perfect are those who are wholehearted in their devotion to God. The hypocrites practice a certain righteousness. They do pious deeds, and their almsgiving is beneficial to others. But their righteousness is not the more abundant righteousness Jesus requires because it comes from a divided loyalty, from an attempt to obtain both the praise of God and the praise of human beings.

Praying in Secret (6:5-6)

Just as there can be a temptation to do charitable works in order to bask in the acclaim and praise of others, so there is a danger that disciples will pray in an ostentatious way in order to gain the attention and acclaim of others. Therefore, after instructing his disciples how to do their charitable deeds secretly, Jesus teaches them to pray in secret as well. The purpose of this teaching is not to forbid the disciples from participating in public prayer and worship. After all, Jesus regularly worshipped in synagogues and, according to the Gospel of John, he went to Jerusalem for the feasts of Passover, Tabernacles, and Dedication. Rather, Jesus contrasts the way in which the hypocrites pray with the manner in which his disciples should pray in order to teach his disciples the difference between being divided and perfect in their devotion to God. The real issue is not public versus private prayer, but a divided versus wholehearted service to God. Whereas the hypocrites pray with hearts divided in their allegiance to God because they seek human praise, Jesus' disciples are to pray with hearts that are perfectly loyal to God. Disciples whose hearts are perfect and whole in their devotion to God will always seek the praise of God rather than of human beings, whether they pray in the presence of others or secretly in their own rooms, as Jesus counsels here.

The structure of this teaching is similar to the structure Jesus employed in his discussion of alms. First, it begins with a warning not to pray in the ostentatious way that the hypocrites do, standing at the corners of streets and synagogues. That the hypocrites stand while they pray is not the problem since standing was a common posture for praying (Mark 11:25; Luke 18:11). Nor is the place where they pray the issue. The issue is the intention of the hypocrites who pray in this way and in these places so that others will see them. Their desire to be seen means that their hearts are no longer pure, for while their prayer is addressed to God, their purpose is to win the praise of human beings. Second, employing the same phrase that he used in his first example, Jesus warns that their reward has been paid in full. There will be no reward for such people at the end of the ages because the human praise they desire and receive is their reward. Third, just as he instructed his disciples to give their alms in secret, he now instructs them to pray in secret, in the privacy of their own room. The admonition to pray secretly and in private is sound advice for disciples who, if they are not careful, can easily fall into the pattern of the hypocrites. In the privacy of one's own room, however, there will be no one to see them but their heavenly Father, thereby forestalling any temptation to seek the praise of others. The injunction to pray in private, then, provides disciples with a way to avoid the temptation to which the hypocrites succumb. For if there is no one to see what the disciples are doing, there is no temptation to seek human praise. Fourth, Jesus concludes with the same reward statement he employed in the first example: their heavenly Father who sees in secret will reward them. The reward that Jesus has in view is an eschatological reward—that is, the reward that will accompany the final appearance of God's kingdom. At that moment what was secret will become apparent to all: that the disciples whom the world hates and despises are the true sons and daughters of Jesus' heavenly Father. Although the world did not see them giving alms or praying, they are the ones whom God claims as the true sons and daughters of the kingdom.

How to Pray (6:7-15)

At this point, Jesus unexpectedly interrupts the pattern of his teaching. Before contrasting the way in which the hypocrites fast with the way his disciples should fast, he provides his listeners with a further teaching on prayer that includes his own prayer, the Lord's Prayer, which occurs at the very center of the Sermon on the Mount. The presence of the Our Father at the midpoint of the sermon highlights its importance and suggests that it should be read in light of the entire sermon and the sermon in light of the prayer so that the prayer and the sermon interpret each other.

Jesus introduces his prayer with a brief statement that contrasts the way in which the Gentiles pray with the way in which his disciples should pray, and he concludes with a further teaching on forgiveness that expands upon the fifth petition in which disciples ask their heavenly Father for forgiveness. The prayer itself begins with an address to God as Father, followed by six petitions. In the first three, disciples pray for what the kingdom of God will bring when it appears in all its power and glory. In the last three, the disciples ask for what is most important for their lives. The material in this teaching is structured in the following way.

> Introduction to the prayer (6:7-8)
> Opening address to God (6:9a)
> Petitions related to God's rule (6:9b-10b)
> > First petition (6:9b)
> > Second petition (6:10a)
> > Third petition (6:10b)
> Petitions related to the disciples' needs (6:11-13)
> > Fourth petition (6:11)
> > Fifth petition (6:12)
> > Sixth petition (6:13)
> Conclusion to the prayer (6:14-15)

Having contrasted the way in which the hypocrites practice their righteousness with the way his disciples are to practice their righteousness, Jesus contrasts the manner in which the Gentiles (those who do not belong to the people of Israel) pray with the way in which his disciples (the nucleus of a renewed Israel) are to pray. Whereas the hypocrites pray to be seen, the Gentiles assault God with a barrage of words and phrases in an attempt to inform and wear down the deity. Ignorant of the God of Israel, whom Jesus calls "Father," the Gentiles pray as if it were necessary to get God's attention and remind God of their needs. Their understanding of prayer, as characterized here, is the more verbose the better the prayer; the longer the prayer the more effective the prayer. Jesus undercuts this understanding of prayer with a simple phrase that he will repeat later: "your Father knows what you need before you ask him" (Matt 6:8, see also 6:32). A similar point is made in Sirach 7:14: "Do not babble in the assembly of the elders, and do not repeat yourself when you pray." Jesus' understanding of prayer is intimately related to his knowledge of God: prayer is addressed to a father who already knows the needs of his children. There is no need, therefore, to assault God with words or to inform God of one's needs. The purpose of prayer is to approach God as a generous Father in order to articulate our needs to ourselves as well as to God. Such prayer makes disciples aware of their true needs of which God is already aware.

The manner in which disciples are to address God in prayer highlights the distinctiveness of the prayer Jesus teaches them. As the Son of God, the one whom the Father identifies as his beloved Son (Matt 3:17), Jesus knows and reveals the Father (Matt 11:27); he is the one who addresses God as "my Father" (Matt 26:39). Because he is the Son of God, Jesus can make his disciples sons and daughters of his heavenly Father. This is why he reminds them throughout the sermon that God is their "Father," their "heavenly Father." This is why they are to give glory to their *Father who is in heaven* by their good works (Matt 5:16) and be perfect as their *heavenly Father* is perfect (Matt 5:48). They are to practice their righteousness in secret so that their *Father* who sees in secret will reward them (Matt 6:4, 6, 18). The secret and the power of the prayer of the disciples, then, is grounded in their understanding of God and Jesus: Jesus is the Son of God who makes them sons and daughters of his heavenly Father.

Since the disciples form a community of disciples that Jesus has created, they address God as "*our* Father," thereby confessing that they belong to the community of those who call God their heavenly Father. This suggests that even when the disciples pray in the secret of their own rooms, they can and should address God as "our Father." In addressing God as their Father, however, the disciples are not making a claim about God's gender, as if God were male rather than female. God is neither male nor female so that to interpret "Father" as a designation of God's gender is to misunderstand what it means to address God as "Father." "Father" is a relational term that expresses the unique relationship between God and Jesus. It conjures up all that is good in the parent-child relationship in order to assure disciples that they can pray to God with complete confidence. An authentic understanding of God as Father then is grounded in an understanding of Jesus as the Son of God. Such an understanding transcends the divisions of gender and focuses on the intimate relationship that exists between Jesus and God and, by analogy, between disciples and their heavenly Father.

The first petition for which disciples pray is the sanctification of God's name ("hallowed be your name"). God's name is holy, and through the divine name God dwells in the midst of his people. To call upon the name of God is to call upon God. The Psalmist exclaims how majestic God's name is (Ps 8:1). It is holy (Ps 30:4); it is glorious (Ps 72:19); and it endures for all generations (Ps 102:12). Because God's name is holy, Israel did not dare speak the name (YHWH) God revealed to Moses at Mount Sinai, replacing it with *Adonai* ("Lord") whenever it occurred in the sacred text. Because the divine name is God's name, it is God who ultimately sanctifies his own name by vindicating himself.

> Therefore say to the house of Israel, Thus says the Lord GOD: It is not for your sake, O house of Israel, that I am about to act, but *for the sake of my holy name*, which you have profaned among the nations to which you came. *I will sanctify my great name*, which has been profaned among the nations, and which you have profaned among them; and the nations shall know that I am the LORD, says the Lord GOD, when through you I display my holiness before their eyes. (Ezek 36:22-23)

In asking God to sanctify his name, disciples pray that God will act in a decisive way that will result in God's final or eschatological victory. When this occurs, God's people will sanctify his name as the book of Isaiah says:

> Therefore thus says the LORD, who redeemed Abraham, concerning the house of Jacob: No longer shall Jacob be ashamed, no longer shall his face grow pale. For when he sees his children, the work of my hands, in his midst, *they will sanctify my name*; *they will sanctify the Holy One of Jacob*, and will stand in awe of the God of Israel. (Isa 29:22-23)

Like the beatitudes, this petition has an eschatological and ethical dimension. On the one hand, it is God who sanctifies his own name by his saving justice that overcomes every evil. On the other, disciples sanctify God's name when they praise and acknowledge how God has sanctified his name.

The second petition ("Your kingdom come") is akin to the first inasmuch as it is God who will bring about the final appearance of the kingdom. To be sure, God's kingdom has made its initial appearance in Jesus' ministry. The mighty deeds that Jesus performs in healing the sick and casting out demons indicate that God's rule is making its appearance. This is why Jesus says to the religious leaders that if he casts out demons by the power of God's Spirit then the kingdom of God has come upon them (Matt 12:28). It is only when Jesus returns at the end of the ages as the glorious Son of Man, however, that the kingdom will appear in all its power and glory in a manner that no one, not even God's enemies, will be able to deny (Matt 13:41-43; 16:28; 25:31). Accordingly, although disciples already experience something of the kingdom in Jesus' ministry, they long for his return and the final appearance of the kingdom at the end of the ages.

This petition, like the first, has an eschatological and ethical dimension. Inasmuch as the kingdom is God's rule over history and creation, only God can bring about its appearance. The kingdom of God is not a human project; nor is it the outcome of society becoming better and better. The kingdom of God is a transcendent reality, a gift from God. Disciples play a role in the coming of the kingdom by proclaiming its presence in the ministry, death, and resurrection of Jesus until he returns in glory (Matt 24:14). They witness to the present reality of the kingdom by practicing the greater righteousness Jesus teaches in the sermon so that others will praise their heavenly Father. By practicing the greater righteousness, they testify to God's rule over their own lives, thereby pointing to the coming rule of God over history and creation that will occur when the kingdom arrives.

The third petition ("Your will be done, on earth as it is in heaven") is closely related to the first two. When the kingdom makes its appearance and God's name is sanctified, this petition will finally be fulfilled inasmuch as the will of God will be done on earth as it is in heaven. To pray that God's will be done on earth as it is in heaven, then, is to pray for the arrival of the kingdom and the sanctification of God's name. Like the first two petitions, this petition has an eschatological and ethical dimension. On the one hand, the will of God will be accomplished with the sanctification of God's name and the final appearance of the kingdom. On the other hand, disciples must *do* God's will here and now as they await the final appearance of the kingdom. This ethical dimension is found in Jesus' warning at the end of the sermon: "Not everyone who says to me, 'Lord, Lord,' will enter the kingdom of heaven, but only the one who does the will of my Father in heaven" (Matt 7:21). Consequently, the true disciple is the one who does God's will. This is why, when he identifies members of his new family, Jesus points to his disciples and says, "For whoever does the will of my Father in heaven is my brother and sister and mother" (Matt 12:50). In doing God's will, Jesus' disciples imitate the example of Jesus. Employing words from his own prayer in the Garden of Gethsemane (Matt 26:42), Jesus prays, "My Father, if this cannot pass unless I drink it, *your will be done.*" There is nothing more important for Jesus and his disciples than doing God's will. In praying that God's will be done, the disciples pray not only for the coming of the kingdom and the sanctification of God's name, they commit themselves to the greater righteousness that Jesus teaches in this sermon—a life of doing God's will.

Having taught his disciples to pray for what is most important in their relationship to God (the sanctification of God's name, the coming of God's kingdom, and the fulfillment of God's will), Jesus next teaches them to pray for what is important for their own lives: the need for the food that will sustain them, the forgiveness of sins, and deliverance from temptation and evil.

Jesus' fourth petition ("Give us this day our daily bread") presents a special problem since it employs a Greek word (*epiousion*) that occurs here and in Luke 11:3 but apparently nowhere else in Greek literature, whose meaning is not clear. It could mean (1) give us the bread that is necessary for human existence, (2) give us the bread that is necessary for today, (3) give us the bread that is necessary for tomorrow, or (4) give us the bread for the future; that is to say, the bread we will eat in the kingdom of God. This is the bread that one of those who dines with Jesus speaks of when he says, "Blessed is anyone who will eat bread in the kingdom of God!" (Luke 14:15). If one interprets Jesus' prayer eschatologically with a view to the final appearance of the kingdom, the fourth meaning is the most appropriate one. But if one interprets the prayer in an ethical manner, anyone of the first three meanings is appropriate. Jesus teaches his disciples to ask their heavenly Father for the food they need to live today and tomorrow and no more. The book of Proverbs offers similar counsel: "give me neither poverty nor riches; feed me with the food that I need" (Prov 30:8). In the next part of the sermon, Jesus will provide his disciples with an extended teaching on the uselessness of anxiety, exhorting them not to worry about what they will eat or drink. If their heavenly Father provides for the birds of the air, he will surely provide for them (Matt 6:25-26). While this ethical interpretation is the one that is most familiar to contemporary believers, the eschatological interpretation should not be overlooked, given the role that the kingdom of God plays in Jesus' prayer and in the sermon.

In the fifth petition ("And forgive us our debts, as we also have forgiven our debtors"), Jesus instructs his disciples to ask their heavenly Father to forgive them in the way they forgive those who are indebted to them. By praying in this way, the disciples invoke the principle of reciprocity inasmuch as they ask God to forgive them *to the extent* that they forgive others. The book of Sirach formulates the principle in this way: "Forgive your neighbor the wrong he has done, and then your sins will be pardoned when you pray" (Sir 28:2).

Jesus' parable of the servant who refused to forgive the debt of a fellow servant after his master had forgiven him an enormous debt he could not possibly repay is the best commentary on this petition (Matt 18:23-34). After telling this parable, Jesus concludes, "So my heavenly Father will also do to every one of you, if you do not forgive your brother or sister from your heart" (18:35). In both the Lord's Prayer and the parable, Jesus likens sin to a debt. But unlike other debts that can be repaid, the debt of sin cannot be repaid by the sinner. Sin is the debt that can only be remitted by the injured party. Accordingly, those who have sinned are dependent upon the forgiveness of those against whom they have sinned. Sin is the debt that can only be remitted by God's grace, the debt that must be repaid by the blood of Christ.

The motivation for disciples to forgive others is their profound awareness that God has already forgiven them an enormous debt they could not repay. If disciples make this petition with an awareness of the debt that has already been forgiven them, they will pray with confidence and hope rather than with fear and trepidation. Those who refuse to forgive others, however, will not be forgiven, not because God is vindictive but because they have forfeited God's forgiveness.

The final petition of Jesus' prayer ("And do not bring us to the time of trial, but rescue us from the evil one") can be interpreted in two ways. On the one hand, if the petition is taken in an eschatological sense, disciples pray that God will rescue them from that great time of testing that will occur when the Evil One (Satan) will test God's saints one last time. For example, before his passion, as he is about to enter the hour of his own great testing, Jesus warns his disciples, "Stay awake and pray that you may not come into the time of trial; the spirit indeed is willing, but the flesh is weak" (Matt 26:41). The testing Jesus has in view here is the great test, the struggle with the Evil One, which he is about to endure. The book of Revelation refers to this final struggle when the risen Christ says to the church at Philadelphia, "Because you have kept my word of patient endurance, I will keep you from *the hour of trial* that is coming on the whole world *to test the inhabitants of the earth*" (Rev 3:10). On the other hand, if the petition is taken in an ethical sense, then Jesus' disciples pray that God will rescue them from the temptations that beset them every day. The letter of James alludes to such temptations when it says, "Blessed is anyone who endures temptation. Such a one has stood the test and will receive the crown of life that the Lord has promised to those who love him" (Jas 1:12). Jesus himself endured such temptation in the wilderness (Luke 4:13).

Although the eschatological interpretation makes the most sense within the context of Matthew's gospel, the ethical sense, which is enshrined in the traditional translation of the Lord's Prayer ("And lead us not into temptation but deliver us from evil"), makes the most sense to contemporary believers. Disciples pray that they will be delivered from the temptations that beset them every day. But in addition to praying that God not lead them into temptation, it is important for disciples to pray that they will be delivered from the final test and struggle with the Evil One, lest they fail and be separated from their Lord.

Before teaching his disciples how to fast, Jesus reinforces the importance of the fifth petition of his prayer with a concluding admonition about the importance of forgiveness. If his disciples forgive the offenses that others have committed against them, their heavenly Father will forgive their offenses; but if they do not forgive the offenses that others have committed against them, neither will their heavenly Father forgive them their offenses. I make two points here. First, whereas in the sixth antithesis Jesus calls upon his disciples to go beyond the law of reciprocity by loving even their enemies, not just those who love them, here he invokes the law of reciprocity. The greater righteousness requires them to forgive those who have sinned against them. The extent to which Jesus' disciples forgive or refuse to forgive others, then, is the measure by which God will or will not forgive them. The reason for this is evident. Since the disciples have already experienced God's forgiveness in Christ, they ought to be all the more ready to forgive others, even those who are unwilling to forgive them. Paul explains this understanding of forgiveness when he writes, "forgive each other; *just as the Lord has forgiven you*, so you also must forgive" (Col 3:13).

Second, although the disciples forgive others, it is possible that others—especially their enemies—will refuse to forgive them. Should this happen, Jesus' disciples can be confident that God will forgive them even if others do not, provided they have forgiven those who have offended them.

Throughout this section, I have suggested that the Lord's Prayer, like the beatitudes, can be prayed in two ways. On the one hand, it can be prayed in terms of its eschatological content; that is, in light of God's coming victory over all that is evil. On the other, it can be prayed in terms of its ethical content, that is, in light of Jesus' teaching on the greater righteousness. When disciples pray the Lord's Prayer in hope of God's coming victory, they pray that God will bring about the sanctification of his name through the final appearance of the kingdom when the will of God shall be done as perfectly on earth as it is already done in heaven. In anticipation of the coming rule of God, disciples pray for the bread of the kingdom, to be forgiven at the last judgment, and to be delivered from the final testing of the Evil One. When disciples pray the Lord's Prayer in light of Jesus' teaching on righteousness, they pray for the grace to sanctify God's name and do God's will so that they may live under God's rule. Because they seek to live under God's rule, they trust in the one who provides them with the sustenance they need. They forgive each other, and they ask God to rescue and protect them from the temptations of everyday life, and so from all evil.

Although these are different ways of praying the Lord's Prayer, they are not opposed to each other, and it is not a matter of choosing one rather than the other. Within the context of the sermon, which anticipates the final appearance of God's kingdom and calls disciples to live by a greater righteousness, the Lord's Prayer has a surplus of meaning that has room for both an eschatological and ethical reading. The in-breaking kingdom of God requires disciples to live a more abundantly righteous life; and that greater righteousness testifies to the coming rule of God.

Fasting in Secret (6:16-18)

Returning to the pattern he established in his teaching on almsgiving and prayer, Jesus contrasts the way in which the hypocrites fast with the manner in which his disciples should fast. First, he notes that when the hypocrites fast they purposely appear sullen and sad (one of the purposes of fasting being to express sorrow) in order to show others that they are fasting. Second, Jesus introduces the same reward statement that he used in his first two examples: the hypocrites have been paid in full, for they have received the reward they sought—the praise and adulation of others. Third, Jesus explains how his disciples are to fast. They should anoint their head with oil as a sign of joy, and they should wash their faces as though they were not fasting (or had just completed a fast). In this way only their heavenly Father will know they are fasting. Fourth, Jesus concludes with the same reward statement he employed in the other examples—and their heavenly Father who sees in secret will reward them.

Fasting played an important role in Israel's life as a way of expressing sorrow, penitence, or preparing for prayer or some other important task. At the beginning of his ministry, for example, Jesus fasts for forty days before inaugurating his ministry (Matt 4:2). During his ministry, however, there are no accounts of Jesus or his disciples fasting. Indeed, he and his disciples are criticized for not fasting (Matt 9:14; 11:18-19). The fact that Jesus teaches his disciples how to fast and that he fasted before beginning his own ministry, however, indicates that he was not adverse to this practice. The real issue is not the value or importance of fasting but how one goes about it. If fasting becomes an occasion for boasting, as it did for the Pharisee who reminded God that he fasted twice a week (Luke 18:12), it loses its value. But if it is done in a way that only God can see, it becomes an expression of the greater righteousness. If Jesus practiced his own teaching and fasted in a way that only his heavenly Father could see, he may have fasted more frequently than others realized and the gospels report.

The central theme of Jesus' teaching on almsgiving, prayer, and fasting is this: whereas the hypocrites practice their piety in a way that reveals they are not wholeheartedly devoted to God, Jesus' disciples are to practice a greater righteousness that expresses its piety in a hidden way that only God can see. The hypocrites are not "perfect" because they perform their piety in a way that seeks the attention and approval of others as well as of God. It is this divided loyalty that prevents them from being perfect and wholehearted in their devotion to God. By instructing his disciples to practice their righteousness in secret, Jesus provides them with a way to become perfect and wholehearted in their allegiance to God: seek only the praise of God. Being perfect, then, is not to be equated with perfectionism. It is not a matter of not making mistakes but of single-minded service and devotion to God. Disciples who are single-minded and wholly devoted to God will make mistakes because they are human, and at times they will fall short of the mark. To the extent they give themselves wholly and entirely to God, however, they will be perfect.

The greater righteousness Jesus teaches in the sermon, and that he requires of his disciples, is a righteousness that seeks the full meaning of God's will as revealed in the Law. It expresses its piety in a hidden way known only to God. Such righteousness can be easily overlooked by others since it is not self-promoting. Exactly how one achieves such single-minded devotion to God is the subject of Jesus' third and final teaching on righteousness, to which we now turn.

Single-Minded Devotion to God 4

Jesus has now provided his disciples with two important teachings on righteousness. In the first, he employed a series of six antitheses to clarify the full meaning of God's will as revealed in the Law. In the second, he exhorted his disciples to practice their acts of righteousness in a hidden way so that their heavenly Father, who sees what they do in secret, will reward them. As Jesus comes to the end of his sermon, he provides his disciples with a third instruction on righteousness that teaches them the need for single-mined devotion to God if they are to practice a greater righteousness. Jesus emphasized the importance of single-minded devotion to God when he told his disciples that they must be perfect as their heavenly Father is perfect (Matt 5:48). He then illustrated what he meant by contrasting the behavior of the hypocrites who practice their piety in order to gain the praise of others with the hidden way in which his disciples are to practice their righteousness. In his third and final teaching on righteousness, Jesus will develop this theme of single-minded devotion to God further.

Whereas it is relatively easy to determine the structure of Jesus' first two teachings on righteousness since the material consists of six antithetical sayings and three sayings on almsgiving, prayer, and fasting that follow a similar pattern, it is more difficult to identify the underlying structure of this third teaching on righteousness. On the one hand, the material consists of seven units:

treasure in heaven (6:19-21), the sound eye (6:22-23), the impossibility of serving two masters (6:24), the uselessness of anxiety (6:25-34), a warning not to judge others (7:1-5), a warning not to give what is holy to those who are not holy (7:6), and an exhortation to pray to God with complete confidence (7:7-11). On the other hand, it is difficult to see how these units are related to each other. Although there is little agreement about the structure of this section, I propose that the material develops the overall theme of the need for single-minded devotion to God in order to practice the righteousness Jesus teaches. Viewed from this perspective, the material can be understood as follows. First, Jesus employs three sayings that emphasize the need to be whole and entire in one's devotion to God (6:19-24). On the basis of this teaching he then exhorts his disciples not to be anxious about their bodily needs since God will provide for them (6:25-34). Finally, in light of what he has said, he gives three examples of what disciples who are wholehearted in their devotion to God should, and should not, do in their daily life (7:1-11). The material of this section can be structured in this way.

1. Single-minded disciples store up treasure in heaven (6:19-21)
2. Single-minded disciples have a sound eye (6:22-23)
3. Single-minded disciples serve one master (6:24)
4. **Single-minded disciples live without worry and anxiety (6:25-34)**
5. Single-minded disciples do not judge each other (7:1-5)
6. Single-minded disciples do not give what is holy to what is not holy (7:6)
7. Single-minded disciples pray to God with total confidence (7:7-11)

According to this structure, the first three sayings provide examples of what it means to be single-minded in one's devotion to God, the fourth unit exhorts those who are single-minded in their devotion to God not to be anxious, and the last three units draw out the consequences of single-minded devotion for everyday life. The hermeneutical key to the material of this section is Matt 6:33, which occurs in the fourth unit: "But strive first for the kingdom of God and its righteousness, and all these things will be given to you as well" (modified NRSV). At the end of this section, Jesus concludes his three teachings on righteousness with a statement commonly referred to as the golden rule (7:12), which echoes what he said earlier at the beginning of his teaching on righteousness about fulfilling the law and the prophets (5:17).

Jesus' first three sayings are closely related to each other inasmuch as their central theme is the need for single-minded devotion to God. In all three sayings, he employs metaphors to communicate what he wants to teach: treasure in heaven, the sound eye, the one master. The exegetical challenge is to determine what Jesus means by these metaphors.

Where Your Treasure Is (6:19-21)

After instructing his disciples how to give alms, pray and fast, Jesus counsels them to store up lasting treasure in heaven. First, he employs a negative imperative to exhort the disciples not to store up treasure for themselves on earth where it can be destroyed and stolen. Next, he employs a positive imperative to exhort them to store their treasure in heaven where it cannot be destroyed or stolen. Finally, he supports his teaching with a keen insight: where people store their treasure reveals the deepest longing of their heart. Accordingly, those who store their treasure on earth, where it can be seen, reveal that they are still living in what Paul calls the realm of the flesh, the sphere of all that is weak, mortal, and so destined for destruction, whereas those who store their treasure in heaven where it cannot be seen have learned to live in the realm of God's Spirit, the sphere of what is immortal, and so destined for eternal life.

In the parable of the rich landowner, Jesus vividly illustrates the folly of storing up treasure on earth (Luke 12:16-21). At the very moment when the landowner determines to tear down his old barns in order to build larger ones to store his abundant wealth, God determines that the landowner will die that very night. Thus Jesus concludes the parable, "So it is with those who store up treasures for themselves but are not rich toward God" (Luke 12:21). Such people may think they are secure, but their security is fleeting and deceiving.

In this teaching on treasure, Jesus contrasts two kinds of treasure: earthly treasure such as the rich landowner piled up for himself and the treasure that is the result of works of righteousness such as almsgiving, prayer, and fasting. Whereas all earthly treasure is subject to decay and theft and must be abandoned at the moment of death, the treasure resulting from one's righteous deeds lasts forever and awaits one after death. Jesus provides the rich young man with similar counsel when he says, "If you wish to be perfect, go, sell your possessions, and give the money to the poor, *and you will have treasure in heaven*; then come, follow me" (Matt 19:21). This treasure that the young man will have—if he heeds Jesus' counsel—will be the result of his almsgiving when he sells his possessions and gives the proceeds to the poor. This relationship between treasure in heaven and deeds of righteousness is illustrated in 2 Esdras, a non-canonical writing of the first century AD. Ezra asks what will happen after death, and he is told, "you have a treasure of works stored up with the Most High, but it will not be shown to you until the last times" (2 Esdras 7:77). Ezra is further told that "the righteous, who have many works laid up with you, shall receive their reward in consequence of their own deeds" (2 Esdras 8:33). The treasure in heaven that Jesus has in view, then, is the result of the greater righteousness to which he summons his disciples.

If Your Eye Is Sound (6:22-23)

Just as he established a contrast between two kinds of treasure, one on earth and the other in heaven, so Jesus establishes a contrast between two kinds of eyes: one that is sound and so produces light, and one that is not sound and so leaves one in darkness. Undergirding this saying is an understanding of vision that differs from our own. Whereas we think of the eye as an organ that sees because it receives light from outside the body, this saying presents the eye as an organ that produces light within the body so that a person can see what is outside the body. This is why Jesus begins with the statement, "the eye is the lamp of the body." On the basis of this understanding of vision, he draws two conclusions. First, if one's eye is sound, then one's whole body will be filled with the light that the eye produces. Second, if one's eye is not sound, then the whole body will be filled with darkness because the eye is no longer able to function as a lamp that illumines the body, enabling one to see.

Although the surface meaning of Jesus' teaching is evident— one must have a sound eye that produces light so that one can see—Jesus is speaking about something more than physical sight. Just as he employed treasure in heaven as a metaphor for the trea- sure that results from deeds of righteousness, so he employs the sound eye as a metaphor for single-minded devotion to God. If disciples are single-minded in their devotion to God, they will be like people with a sound and healthy eye whose bodies are filled with light. In contrast to them the hypocrites, whose allegiance is divided, are like people with an unhealthy eye whose bodies are filled with darkness. If this is the meaning of Jesus' teaching, there is a close relationship between this and the previous teach- ing. Those who store their treasure in heaven are people with a sound eye because they are single-minded in their devotion to God, whereas those who store their treasure on earth are people with an unsound eye because, like the rich young man, they are divided in their allegiance. They seek eternal life, but they are unwilling to follow the way of perfection.

The book of Sirach employs the "evil eye" as a metaphor for the miser: "An *evil eye* begrudges bread, and it is lacking at his table" (Sir 14:10; modified NRSV). Jesus employs a similar expres- sion in his parable of the workers in the vineyard (Matt 20:1-16). When the first workers complain that the last have been paid the same wage as they received, the owner of the vineyard replies, "Am I not allowed to do what I choose with what belongs to me? Or is *your eye evil* because I am generous?" (Matt 20:15; modified NRSV). In his letter to the Ephesians, Paul employs the eye as a positive metaphor when he writes, "I pray that the God of our Lord Jesus Christ, the Father of glory, may give you a spirit of wisdom and revelation as you come to know him, so that, *with the eyes of your heart enlightened,* you may know what is the hope to which he has called you, what are the riches of his glorious inheritance among the saints" (Eph 1:17-18). The sound or healthy eye, then, is a metaphor for wholehearted, single-minded devotion to God. It points to those who are generous in spirit because they understand God's will and are totally committed to it. Those whose eye is sound are perfect as their heavenly Father is perfect.

Only One Master (6:24)

Whereas in his first two teachings Jesus made use of metaphors (treasure in heaven, the sound eye) that his disciples had to decode, in his third teaching he decodes the metaphor for them. His teaching begins with a thesis statement: no one can serve two masters. Next, he provides a supporting reason for his thesis: it is not possible to give both masters the same degree of loyalty and devotion. Even if one feels an allegiance to both, one will eventually prefer one to the other. Finally, Jesus decodes his own teaching by identifying the two masters as God and money ("mammon" in many translations). Because one will always be more devoted to one master than to another, one must eventually choose between competing lords.

For those who lived in a world where slavery was the engine that drove the economy of the day, Jesus' teaching would have made perfect sense. Masters require absolute loyalty and obedience from their slaves. Therefore, just as slaves must serve their masters with total devotion, so disciples must serve their Lord with undivided allegiance. Paul makes a similar point in Romans 6, when he reminds his audience that just as they once presented every part of their body in service to the power of sin, so—now that they have been incorporated into Christ—they must present the parts of their bodies as slaves of righteousness in total devotion to God. In the Gospel of Luke, Jesus employs the same saying to explain the correct use of possessions (Luke 16:13). One cannot be wholly devoted to God if one is fully devoted to the pursuit of wealth; one must choose between the two.

Like the previous two sayings, this teaching highlights the need for Jesus' disciples to be single-minded in their service to God. In doing so, it provides a fitting climax to the first two statements. Having exhorted his disciples to store up treasure in heaven by investing in imperishable works of righteousness rather than the perishable wealth of this world, and having told them that they must be single-minded in their devotion to God, Jesus explains that they can serve only one master. All three sayings, then, make the same point. Treasure in heaven, the sound eye, and serving one master are metaphors for the need to be wholehearted in one's devotion to God. Like Jesus' teaching on almsgiving, prayer, and fasting, which encouraged the disciples to be wholehearted in their service to God, these three teachings explain what it means to be perfect. Those who are perfect are single-minded in their devotion to God.

Do Not Be Anxious (6:25-34)

Having provided his disciples with three teachings on the need to be single-minded in their devotion to God, Jesus exhorts them not to be anxious for their bodily needs. By beginning his teaching with "therefore," he indicates that what he is about to say is closely related to what he has just said: if his disciples are intent on storing up treasure for themselves in heaven, and if they are single-minded in their devotion to God as their sole master, then they will understand that there is no need to be anxious about their lives. They will comprehend that those who are totally devoted to God place all their trust in God.

Jesus' teaching on the folly of anxiety presents an enduring challenge to disciples of every age. Before discussing the practicality of his teaching, however, it will be helpful to examine the logic of his discourse. Why does Jesus exhort his disciples not to be anxious? What arguments does he marshal for his teaching? Most importantly, what does this teaching reveal about his understanding of God? The material in this section is structured around three negative imperatives: "Do not worry."

> **A first negative imperative not to worry (6:25a)**
> Supporting arguments from nature (6:25b-30)
>> Rhetorical question about what is important (6:25b)
>> God feeds the birds (6:26a)
>> Rhetorical question about who is more important (6:26b)
>> Rhetorical question about worrying (6:27)
>> Rhetorical question about clothing (6:28a)
>> God clothes the grass of the field (6:28b-29)
>> Rhetorical question about the lilies (6:30)
> **A second negative imperative not to worry (6:31)**
> Supporting reasons (6:32)
>> This is what the Gentiles do (6:32a)
>> God knows what you need (6:32b)
> What to seek: the kingdom and its righteousness (6:33)
> **A third negative imperative not to worry (6:34a)**
> Supporting reason for not worrying (6:34b)

Jesus begins his teaching with his first negative imperative that covers those aspects of daily life (food, drink, and clothing) that cause most people to worry and be anxious: "Therefore I tell you, do not worry about your life, what you will eat or what you will drink, or about your body, what you will wear" (6:25a). Although it is easy to say this to those who live in an affluent society, how can one responsibly say this to those who live from day to day, not knowing if there will be food or clothing tomorrow?

In response to this objection, Jesus provides an extended argument that consists of examples from nature and several rhetorical questions (6:25b-30). The first part of his argument is in the form of a rhetorical question that puts everything in perspective (6:25b).

As important as food and drink are, life is more important. And as important as clothing is, the body is more important. In other words, since God has already provided his children with what is most important—what they cannot give themselves—those who are single-minded in their devotion to God should trust that God will give the food and drink necessary to sustain life and the clothing necessary to adorn the body. To be anxious about food, drink, and clothing, then, is to overlook what is most important: life and the body.

Next, Jesus turns to an example from nature (6:26a) that he follows with yet another rhetorical question (6:26b). Unlike humans who plant and store their crops, the birds that one sees every day never provide for their future. They do not plant, they do not harvest, they do not gather food into barns for the future, and yet they do not go hungry because the one whom the disciples call their heavenly Father feeds them every day. Arguing from what is less important to what is more important, Jesus asks yet another rhetorical question: "How much more valuable are you than the birds?" (6:26b). In other words, if the disciples truly believe that it is God who cares for the birds of the air, they can be all the more confident that God will care for them. One may, of course, object that God does not really feed the birds of the air. One may object that there are creatures that die every day for lack of food, thereby proving Jesus is wrong. But such objections miss the point of Jesus' argument, which is grounded in an understanding of God who is ever concerned for his creation. Put another way, if one thinks of God as removed and unconcerned for creation, this argument makes little sense. But this is not Jesus' understanding of God. As the Son of God, Jesus knows that God is concerned about and cares for every creature.

Having shown his disciples that they should not be anxious about what they will eat and drink since God, who provides for the birds of the air, will surely provide for them, in the next part of his discourse Jesus turns to the question of clothing. To make his argument, he begins with a rhetorical question that highlights the uselessness of worry and anxiety: "And can any of you by worrying add a single hour to your span of life?" (6:27). Once more, Jesus' question gets to the core of the issue. Anxiety accomplishes nothing. Worrying about the extent of one's life does not increase the length of one's life—indeed, it may even shorten it. To worry and be anxious about what might happen changes nothing. Rather than worry, disciples should trust in their heavenly Father. For only their heavenly Father, the giver of life, can extend life.

Jesus follows this rhetorical question with yet another question that introduces a second example from nature: "And why are you anxious about clothing?" (6:28a). Pointing to the lilies of the field, he argues that even though the lilies do not make their own clothing, not even the great king Solomon was more beautifully adorned than they. Just as God provides food for the birds of the air, so God provides clothing for the flowers of the field. Employing the same kind of reasoning he used earlier, Jesus argues from the lesser to the greater. Since God so clothes the lilies, which are here today and gone tomorrow, with such extravagant beauty, will God not provide all the more for his children? This time, however, Jesus addresses his disciples as men of "little faith," thereby highlighting the real problem. It is not that the disciples do not believe; they do. The problem is the nature of their faith. They have not resolved the tension between faith and fear, trust, and anxiety. On the one hand, the disciples believe in Jesus as the Messiah, the Son of the Living God, as Peter's confession shows (Matt 16:16). On the other, they are still fearful and afraid. For example, when Jesus rescues them from a storm at sea, he asks, "Why are you afraid, you of little faith?" (Matt 8:26). When Jesus calls the disciples men of "little faith," then, he indicates that their faith is not yet perfect because they are fearful and anxious.

Having shown his disciples that they are not to be anxious about food or clothing because God will provide for them, Jesus introduces a second negative imperative that draws a conclusion from all that he has said thus far: "Therefore do not worry, saying, 'What will we eat?' or 'What will we drink?' or 'What will we wear?'" (6:31). This time, however, he provides his disciples with a different argument: these are the things about which the Gentiles—

who do not know the God of Israel and the Father of Jesus—are concerned. They are not the things about which disciples should concern themselves. The argument Jesus employs here is similar to the reasoning he used when teaching his disciples how to pray. Earlier he said they are not to pray as the Gentiles who pile up words as if they had to wear down and inform God of their needs. Here he argues that the Gentiles worry about these things as if God were not aware of their needs, or could not provide for them. The central issue, then, is God. Whereas the Gentiles approach God as distant and remote from their needs, Jesus approaches God as a heavenly Father who provides for the needs of his children.

The antidote to the behavior of the Gentiles, Jesus says, is to "strive first for the kingdom of God and its righteousness, and all these things will be given to you as well" (6:33, modified NRSV). With this statement, Jesus provides his disciples with the perfect definition of what it means to be single-minded in devotion to God so that one will be perfect as the heavenly Father is perfect. What the disciples ought to seek above all else is the kingdom of God that Jesus makes possible through his ministry and the righteousness that is appropriate to the kingdom. This is what is most important, and if this counsel is pursued all else will fall into place. Disciples who store up treasure in heaven understand this. Disciples whose eye is sound pursue the kingdom. Disciples who serve only God live lives of righteousness. Those who seek the kingdom and its righteousness are not to be anxious about what is secondary. They choose what is most important, the kingdom of God, with the knowledge that if they enter the kingdom all else will follow.

Jesus concludes this teaching with a third and final negative imperative: "So do not worry about tomorrow" (6:34a), which he supports with the following reasoning, "for tomorrow will bring worries of its own. Today's trouble is enough for today" (6:34b). Whereas in the first two negative imperatives, Jesus told his disciples not to be anxious about food and clothing, now he instructs them not to be anxious about what will happen tomorrow. The advice he gives can be paraphrased in this way: Live one day at a time. Why worry about the anxieties that tomorrow will bring since every day brings its own problems? Deal with problems as they come rather than before they arrive. While this is good practical advice, it also echoes what Jesus said in his prayer: "Give us this day our daily bread." The true disciple lives day by day, trusting in God's provident care.

The extraordinary teaching that Jesus gives in this section finds echoes in both the Old and New Testament. For example, the Psalmist writes, "Cast your burden upon the LORD, and he will sustain you; he will never permit the righteous to be moved" (Ps 55:22). And Paul exhorts the Philippians, "Do not worry about anything, but in everything by prayer and supplication with thanksgiving let your requests be made known to God" (Phil 4:6). Such advice, however, is easier to give than to observe, which raises the question of the "practicality" of Jesus' teaching. Will God really provide for those who entrust themselves to his provident care? Can one responsibly tell those who lack the basic necessities of life to trust in God and all will be well?

There is no simple answer to this question, and the fact that countless people die every day for lack of food and clothing seems to contradict Jesus' teaching. Without pretending to resolve this problem, I make two points. First, as is so often the case in the Sermon on the Mount, it is important not to turn Jesus' words into a set of rules and commandments. Jesus does not so much legislate as he provides his disciples with a new understanding of God that, if followed, will radically change and transform their lives. Second, the truth of Jesus' teaching must be experienced. Put another way, the truth of what he teaches can only be known by those who put it into practice. For every argument against the practicality of what Jesus teaches, there is the witness of those who have confirmed his teaching by their lives. The lives of people such as Francis of Assisi and Mother Teresa can tell us if this teaching is true.

Do Not Judge (7:1-5)

Thus far, in his third great teaching on righteousness, Jesus has emphasized the need for single-minded service to God, which he characterizes as seeking the kingdom of God and the righteousness that is appropriate to it. If his disciples live in this way, they will not be anxious about their lives: what they are to eat, what they are to wear. In the final part of this teaching on righteousness, Jesus draws out three conclusions from what he has said thus far: disciples should not judge each other; disciples must protect what is holy; disciples should pray to their heavenly Father with total confidence.

Jesus begins this teaching, as he often does in the sermon, with a negative imperative that leaves no doubt about his intention: the disciples are *not* to judge lest they be judged (7:1). Next, he provides his disciples with a supporting reason for this imperative: the manner in which they judge will be the manner in which they will be judged, and the measure they measure (what they give to others) will be the measure they will receive (7:2). Next, Jesus asks two rhetorical questions that disclose the hypocrisy of those who judge others (7:3-4). He then concludes this teaching with a positive imperative in which he warns those who judge others to attend to their own faults first (7:5).

Earlier in his teaching on prayer, Jesus taught his disciples to ask their heavenly Father to forgive them as they have forgiven others, warning them that if they do not forgive others, their heavenly Father will not forgive them. Now he provides his disciples with an analogous teaching on judgment: they should not judge each other lest they be judged; for they will be judged by the kind of judgment they pronounce against each other. In issuing this warning, Jesus reveals his understanding of the human person. Although disciples may think they are in a position to judge each other fairly and justly, this is rarely the case. Human judgment is flawed because it cannot fully understand the heart and motives of the other. Moreover, those who judge others rarely understand their own motives and faults. Only God sees the heart and understands. Only God can judge justly. Accordingly, disciples are warned to avoid all judgment to the extent this is possible lest they be judged in the way they judge.

In his great letter to the Romans, Paul provides a similar teaching. After describing the sinful condition of humanity apart from God's grace, he addresses an imaginary interlocutor who approves of what Paul has just said but does the same things: "Therefore you have no excuse, whoever you are, when you judge others; for in passing judgment on another you condemn yourself, because you, the judge, are doing the very same things" (Rom 2:1). Like Jesus, Paul understands that those who judge others put themselves at risk since they often do the very things they condemn others for doing. Consequently, toward the end of this same letter, he asks those members of the Roman community who are judging others, "Who are you to pass judgment on servants of another? It is before their own lord that they stand or fall. And they will be upheld, for the Lord is able to make them stand" (Rom 14:4). James makes a similar point when he writes, "Do not speak evil against one another, brothers and sisters. Whoever speaks evil against another or judges another, speaks evil against the law and judges the law; but if you judge the law, you are not a doer of the law but a judge" (Jas 4:11; see also 5:9).

Jesus employs two rhetorical questions, each one making use of hyperbole, to show how difficult it is for human beings to judge each other rightly. In the first question, he notes that it is always easier for people to see the faults of others than to recognize their own failings, even when their failings are greater than the faults they condemn in others (7:3). In the second, he asks how one can correct the faults of others when one's own failings prevent one from seeing clearly (7:4). Jesus' use of "brother" in both texts suggests that he has in view the correction of a fellow disciple.

But what of Jesus' teaching in Matthew 18, where he provides his disciples with a procedure for correcting a fellow disciple within the community of the church (Matt 18:15-20)? Is Jesus contradicting himself by commanding his disciple to do something there that he forbids here? Not necessarily. Whereas here Jesus is talking about the danger of *judging* others, in Matthew 18 he provides his disciples with a way of *correcting* others within the community of the church. The difference, then, is between correction and judgment. While there are moments when disciples must correct fellow disciples within the community of the church for the sake of the church and each other's salvation, disciples should refrain from that kind of judging that has nothing to do with building up the church or bringing others to salvation because it is primarily concerned with making negative statements about others.

In the final part of this teaching, Jesus addresses those who would judge others with the same harsh terms that he used to describe those who practice their righteousness for others to see. Like those who practice almsgiving, prayer, and fasting for the sake of human praise, those who judge others are hypocrites since their own faults are as great as, if not greater than, the faults they condemn (7:5). Those who would judge others must first remove the "log" from their own eye. Only then will they see clearly enough to remove the "speck" from their brother's eye. The manner in which Jesus uses the eye in this teaching and his identification of those who judge as "hypocrites" highlights the relationship between this teaching and the central theme of this section: the need for single-minded devotion to God. Those who judge others are like the hypocrites who are not wholehearted in their devotion to God because their eye is not sound. On first appearance, they may appear to be single-minded in their devotion to God, but on closer examination they are not. The fact that they do not recognize their own faults reveals that their eye is not sound–they are not wholehearted in their devotion to God. Judging others, then, is a symptom of a divided heart because it is not concerned with the good and well-being of others but with one's superiority to the other.

Protecting What Is Holy (7:6)

Jesus has made use of two important metaphors in this third teaching on righteousness: treasure in heaven and the sound eye. Whereas he employed treasure in heaven as a metaphor for works of righteousness, he used the sound eye as a metaphor for wholehearted service to God. In a brief but enigmatic saying, Jesus now introduces two statements that also make use of metaphors: "Do not give what is holy to dogs; and do not throw your pearls before swine, or they will trample them under foot and turn and maul you." This saying begins with two negative imperatives ("do not give . . . do not throw"), and it concludes with two consequences ("they will trample them . . . and maul you"). The literal meaning of the saying is clear: it is foolish to give what is holy to those who do not understand or appreciate it. There are two sayings in the book of Proverbs that make a similar point: "A scoffer who is rebuked will only hate you; the wise, when rebuked, will love you" (Prov 9:8). "Do not speak in the hearing of a fool, who will only despise the wisdom of your words" (Prov 23:9). The point of these proverbs is clear: Trying to rebuke an insolent person or speak wisdom to a fool is a waste of time since such people are not receptive to correction and wisdom. Indeed, they are more likely to turn on those who seek to correct and instruct them than they are to learn from them. Although the literal meaning of this saying is apparent, its meaning within the Sermon on the Mount and its relationship to Jesus' teaching on single-minded service to God is not. The exegetical challenge, then, is to determine the metaphorical meaning of dogs, pearls, and swine in order to understand how this saying coheres with Jesus' teaching in the rest of the sermon.

For Jesus and his Jewish contemporaries, dogs and swine were unclean animals. Thus it is not surprising that when Jesus heals two men possessed by demons, the demons beg him to send them into a herd of swine since they want to dwell in what is unclean (Matt 8:31). Later, when a Gentile woman implores Jesus to heal her daughter who is tormented by a demon, Jesus harshly replies, "It is not fair to take the children's food and throw it to the dogs" (Matt 15:26). The meaning of this harsh saying is that since Jesus' primary mission is to his own people, the lost sheep of the house of Israel (Matt 15:24), it is not right for him at this point in his ministry to take the "bread" (the gospel of the kingdom) and give it to the "dogs" (the Gentiles who are unclean because they lack the Law of Moses). Nonetheless, Jesus does heal the woman's daughter and, after his resurrection from the dead, he sends his disciples to preach the gospel to all the nations (Matt 28:19). During his earthly ministry, however, he restricts his mission to the people of

Israel. Finally, in his parables on the kingdom of heaven, Jesus tells the parable of a merchant in search of fine pearls (Matt 13:45-45). When the merchant finds a pearl of great value, he sells all that he has in order to purchase it. Within the context of Jesus' other parables, it is apparent that the pearl of great price, for which all else should be sold, is the kingdom of heaven.

In light of the way that Jesus employs these metaphors in the rest of Matthew's gospel, the above saying could be interpreted as follows. The message of the kingdom is the pearl of great price—what is truly holy. While the gospel of the kingdom must be preached to all the nations, those who preach it must take care to guard it as well. When Jesus sends his disciples on mission, therefore, he tells them that if any town does not receive them, they are to go into the streets and say, "Even the dust of your town that clings to our feet, we wipe off in protest against you" (Luke 10:11). While the gospel is to be preached to all, there are those who will trample it under foot and attack those who announce it. Therefore, disciples must take care to protect the message of the kingdom. On the one hand, they are to proclaim the gospel of the kingdom to all nations (Matt 28:19-20). But on the other hand, they are not to be so foolish as to hand on the mysteries of the kingdom to those who will only mock and ridicule these precious mysteries. Jesus himself, for example, reveals the mysteries of the kingdom to his disciples, but speaks to the crowds in parables because they see but do not perceive; they hear but they do not understand (13:11-13).

Asking with Confidence (7:7-11)

Jesus' final teaching in this section returns to the theme of prayer and is closely related to his discourse on the folly of worry and anxiety. As he did in his teaching on prayer, Jesus reminds his disciples that they are praying to a heavenly Father who is always receptive to their needs. And as he did in his discourse on worry and anxiety, he focuses their attention on God's provident care for them. What Jesus says here, then, is closely related to his overall theme of wholehearted service to God. Those who are perfect and single-minded in their service to God will approach their heavenly Father with complete confidence that God will grant what they ask.

Jesus begins his teaching with three imperatives (7:7). *Ask* and you will receive. *Search* and you will find what you are seeking. *Knock* and the door will be opened for you. To support this statement, he affirms that those who ask, receive; those who search, find; and for those who knock, the door is opened (7:8). Taken in isolation, these statements make little sense, and they hardly correspond to what people experience in their everyday relations with each other. People rarely receive what they ask for; they do not always find what they seek; and the door does not always open when one knocks. But Jesus is referring to something entirely different. He has in view the new way in which his disciples must trust in God as their heavenly Father. Such trust enables disciples to pray with the confidence that God will grant what they ask for in faith. Jesus makes a similar statement later when he says, "Whatever you ask in prayer with faith, you will receive" (Matt 21:22; see also 18:19).

To undergird his premise Jesus offers two examples from everyday life (7:9-10). A loaf of bread in ancient Galilee might have the shape of a stone, but would a father give his son a stone if he asked for bread? And a fish from the Sea of Galilee might look like a snake, but would a father give his son a snake if he asked for a fish? These questions require no answers since everyday experience teaches people that parents do not behave in this way when dealing with their children. On the basis of this everyday experience, Jesus draws a conclusion that moves from the lesser to the greater (7:11). If human beings, who are evil, know how to give good gifts to their children, then it is all the more certain that the heavenly Father who is all good will give good things to those who ask.

Someone, of course, might object that our everyday experience of prayer belies this since we do not always receive what we ask for in prayer. Two points need to be made here. First and most importantly, Jesus speaks out of his own experience, which he shares with those whom he makes sons and daughters of his heavenly Father. Those who are wholehearted and single-minded in their devotion to God, as is Jesus, will know the truth of these words. Those who are not will be puzzled by them. Second, Jesus says that his heavenly Father knows how to give "good gifts" to those who ask, the implication being that God gives only *good* gifts. Those who do not ask rightly, then, will not receive what they ask for. James makes this point when he writes, "You ask and do not receive, because you ask wrongly, in order to spend what you get on your pleasures" (Jas 4:3).

The Law and the Prophets (7:12). At the end of his three great teachings on righteousness, Jesus summarizes the essence of what he has said in a saying that has come to be known as the golden rule: "In everything do to others as you would have them do to you; for this is the law and the prophets." This saying has a parallel in Tob 4:15 ("what you hate, do not do to anyone") and Sir 31:15 ("Judge your neighbor's feelings by your own, and in every matter be thoughtful"). It is also found in writings outside of the Bible. Thus one could say that the golden rule expresses common human wisdom: treat others in the way that you would want them to treat you. But Jesus gives this saying a new dimension by relating it to the Law and the Prophets and using it as a summary of his teaching on righteousness. The essence of the Law and the Prophets is the love commandment as Jesus tells the scribe who asks him what is the greatest and first commandment. After answering the scribe that the first commandment is to love God and the second is to love one's neighbor, Jesus concludes, "On these two commandments hang all the *law and the prophets*" (Matt 22:40). Although Jesus does not cite both commandments here, what he has said throughout the sermon indicates that the essence of the Law and the Prophets is found in love for God and neighbor.

At the outset of his teaching on righteousness, Jesus says that he did not come to destroy the *Law or the Prophets* (5:17), and at the conclusion of his teaching on righteousness he says that the

Law and the Prophets is a matter of doing to others what you want them to do to you. By referring to the Law and the Prophets at the beginning and at the end of his teaching on righteousness, Jesus brackets his teaching on the greater righteousness between two important sayings about the Law and the Prophets. What Jesus has taught finds its fulfillment in the love commandment: it does not contradict or do away with the Law and the Prophets. Those who obey Jesus' teaching will practice the Law and the Prophets in a way that reveals their deepest meaning as the six antitheses have shown (5:21-48). They will practice acts of righteousness with a singled-minded devotion that avoids all hypocrisy as Jesus' teaching on prayer, almsgiving and fasting has shown (6:1-18). They will live their lives in wholehearted service to God as Jesus' teaching on true treasure, the sound eye, serving one master, avoiding worry, not judging others, protecting what is holy, and praying with confidence has shown (6:19–7:11). This is the fulfillment of the Law and the Prophets.

The Need to Do Jesus' Words 5

Jesus concludes his great sermon with an extended exhortation that emphasizes the importance of doing what he has taught. This exhortation dispels any notion that the sermon is an impossible ethic. What Jesus has taught is the way his disciples are meant to live. There is no question about the practicality of his teaching. Jesus does not intend his teaching for a select few who are seeking to be perfect. The way of perfection as described in this sermon is meant for all disciples without exception. The question about the practicality of the sermon, which has been debated throughout the centuries, is not a concern for Jesus. The righteousness he describes in his sermon is the way those who have embraced the kingdom of God are to practice their discipleship. The single-minded, wholehearted devotion to God that characterized Jesus' own life is the manner of life that every disciple, without exception, must embrace. In St. Augustine's words, the sermon is the perfect measure of the Christian life, the norm by which disciples measure themselves as disciples. If we ask how this is possible, the answer is found in Jesus' message of the in-breaking kingdom of God. Those who have embraced this message and placed themselves under God's rule understand the demands of the new life the kingdom brings. Having embraced that life, they discover that being under God's rule enables them to live in a way they once thought impossible. They soon learn that by living in a community of like-minded disciples they can do what they once thought impossible; they can live lives of superior righteousness.

The conclusion to the sermon, in which Jesus exhorts his disciples to do what he has taught, has three parts. First, Jesus employs the familiar metaphor of the two ways to exhort his disciples to enter through the narrow gate (7:13-14). Second, he warns them of false prophets who appear like sheep but are really ravenous wolves. Although these prophets call Jesus "Lord," they will be excluded from the kingdom because they do not practice the righteousness he has taught (7:15-23). Finally, Jesus returns to the theme of the two ways by contrasting two kinds of builders, one who is wise and one who is foolish (7:24-27). After Jesus finishes delivering this sermon, Matthew records the reaction of the crowds who have heard Jesus' teaching (7:28-29), thereby echoing the description of the disciples and crowd who gathered to hear the sermon (5:1-2).

The conclusion to the sermon is important for understanding how Jesus wants his words to be heard. He presents his teaching as the path to life. Those who merely admire his teaching from afar or praise it for its insight misunderstand its purpose. Because Jesus teaches in order to bring people to life, it is imperative for those who hear his sermon to *do* the words of the sermon. Hearing without doing is of no avail. Jesus' disciples and all who would be his disciples must be doers of the Word.

The Two Ways (7:13-14)

Jesus begins with a metaphor that contrasts two gates, one that is narrow and one that is wide. Each gate is the entrance to a road, one that is easy to follow but leads to destruction, the other that is difficult to travel but leads to life. While many find the wide gate that leads to the road that is easy to travel, only a few find the narrow gate and the difficult road that leads to life. This metaphor of the two ways was well known to Jesus' contemporaries. For example, toward the end of the book of Deuteronomy, after presenting Israel with the Law, Moses sets a stark choice before the people: "I call heaven and earth to witness against you today that I have set before you life and death, blessings and curses. Choose life so that you and your descendants may live" (Deut 30:19). Employing a similar metaphor, Psalm 1 opens the book of Psalms by describing two ways of life. Contrasting the righteous who delight in the Law of the Lord with the wicked who do not observe the Law, the Psalm compares the righteous to trees planted by streams of water that bear fruit and the wicked to the chaff that is driven by the wind. One of the most important and detailed expositions of the two ways, however, occurs in the *Didache*, an early Christian writing, which begins, "There are two ways, one of life and one of death, and there is a great difference between these two ways" (1:1).[1] In describing the way of life, the *Didache* echoes material found in the Sermon on the Mount. For example, it says, "The teaching of these words is this: Bless those who curse you, and pray for your enemies, and fast for those who persecute you. For what credit is it if you love those who love you? Do not even the Gentiles do the same? But you must love those who hate you, and you will not have an enemy" (1:3). According to the *Didache*, the teaching of the Sermon on the Mount is the way of life.

In the Sermon on the Mount, the metaphor of the narrow gate refers to the teaching that Jesus has just given: the way of righteousness that surpasses the righteousness of the scribes and Pharisees. This is the narrow gate through which one enters the difficult path that leads to life. It is the gate that is difficult to find because it requires single-minded service and wholehearted devotion to God. It is the path that is hard to travel because such wholehearted service requires disciples to give their entire allegiance to God. If the metaphor of the narrow gate refers to Jesus' teaching on righteousness, the metaphor of the wide gate refers to a life of lawlessness. This gate is wide and the way is easy because it does not require people to practice righteousness. The lawless do as they wish without regard for God's will.

Toward the end of the gospel, Jesus contrasts two ways of life when he describes his return as the royal Son of Man at the end of the ages (Matt 25:31-46). He says that at that moment, he will separate the sheep from the goats on the basis of what people have done or failed to do to the least of those who belong to him (Matt 25:40). The narrow gate, then, is a metaphor for doing what Jesus teaches, whereas the wide gate is a metaphor for conduct that does not correspond to his teaching.

The most surprising aspect of this metaphor, however, is Jesus' statement that while many enter through the wide gate, only a few find the narrow gate. Jesus makes a similar point at the end of the parable of the wedding banquet when he says, "For many are called, but few are chosen" (Matt 22:14). With this remark, he warns disciples of every age that while the gospel will be preached to all the nations (Matt 28:19) and while all are called to the wedding banquet of the kingdom, entrance into the life of the kingdom is not to be taken for granted. Although God's offer of salvation is completely gracious, it requires a response. This response is the way of righteousness as described in the Sermon on the Mount, a way of perfect obedience and single-minded service to God. Such a way, Jesus warns, is difficult to find, and few discover it because they are unwilling to give their complete allegiance to the one who calls them. But for those who find it, the narrow gate leads to life.

False Prophets (7:15-23)

Although it may appear from the previous metaphor that it is easy to discern the difference between the way to life and the way to death, Jesus' warning about false prophets indicates that external appearances can be deceiving. It is not possible to judge the interior disposition of people from their exterior actions since people can act hypocritically. People may appear to have entered through the narrow gate, and it may seem they are on the way to life, but closer examination shows that they have entered through the wide gate and are on the road to destruction.

Jesus' warning about false prophets has two parts. In the first, he warns his disciples of the false prophets who will arise in their midst when he is no longer present (7:15-20). In the second, he describes how he will respond to these false prophets on the

Day of Judgment (7:21-23). Jesus provides his disciples with this warning to reinforce what he has said throughout the sermon: appearances are deceiving. The true prophet is not necessarily the one who performs mighty deeds and calls Jesus "Lord," but the one who does the righteousness Jesus teaches in this sermon.

The first part of Jesus' teaching begins with a warning to beware of false prophets, for while they may appear to belong to the community of Jesus' disciples they are enemies of his flock (7:15). Jesus has already warned his disciples to "beware" of practicing their piety for others to see (6:1), and he will warn them to "beware" of the "yeast" (the teaching) of the Pharisees and scribes (Matt 16:6, 11, 12) since their actions do not correspond to their interior dispositions (Matt 23:25, 27-28). Following this warning, he employs the metaphor of a tree and the fruit that it bears to provide disciples with a way to discern true and false prophets. Just as one knows a tree by the kind of fruit it bears, so one can distinguish true and false prophets by the fruit they produce (7:16-20).

The metaphor that Jesus employs here occurs several times in the Gospel of Matthew. For example, when John the Baptist sees the Pharisees and Sadducees coming for his baptism, he calls them a "brood of vipers" and warns them to "bear fruit worthy of repentance" because the Day of Judgment is at hand. On that day every tree that does not bear good fruit will be cut down and thrown into the fire (Matt 3:7-10). At the outset of this gospel, then, John the Baptist compares the Pharisees and Sadducees to rotten trees because they have not borne the fruit of repentance. They have not followed the way of righteousness that he has shown them (Matt 21:32). Although they come to him to be baptized, John recognizes their hypocrisy because he is a true prophet; indeed he is more than a prophet (Matt 11:9).

Shortly after delivering the Sermon on Mount, Jesus has his own encounter with the Pharisees who accuse him of casting out demons by Beelzebul, the ruler of demons (Matt 12:24). In response to their accusation, he employs the metaphor of the tree once more (Matt 12:33-37). If the Pharisees want to bear good fruit, they must become like a good tree, for "the good person brings good things out of a good treasure, and the evil person brings evil things out of an evil treasure" (Matt 12:35). In Jesus' estimation the Pharisees are evil and incapable of speaking what is good.

Jesus also employs the fruit metaphor in the parable of the tenants (Matt 21:33-44). Telling the parable in the presence of the chief priests and Pharisees, he warns them that the kingdom of God will be taken away from them and given to a people "that produces the fruits of the kingdom" (Matt 21:43). Although Jesus does not specify what he means by "the fruits of the kingdom," what he has said throughout the gospel indicates that he is speaking of righteousness: conduct in accord with God's will. Like the tenant farmers who were entrusted with a vineyard but failed to give its owner the fruit of the harvest, the religious leaders were entrusted with the vineyard of the Lord—the people of Israel—but they failed to bring forth a harvest of righteousness. Jesus' disciples, then, will be able to discern true prophets from false prophets by the fruit they bear. Those prophets who live lives of righteousness that correspond with what Jesus teaches are true prophets, whereas those who do not exhibit lives of righteousness are false prophets, no matter how powerful their works.

In the second part of his teaching, Jesus reveals how he will respond to the false prophets on the Day of Judgment (7:21-23). First, he cautions that not everyone who addresses him as "Lord" will gain admittance to the kingdom of heaven, but only those who do the will of his Father. Second, he says that even though people will protest that they prophesied in his name, expelled demons in his name, and performed powerful deeds in his name, Jesus will reject them on the Day of Judgment with these harsh words: "I never knew you; go away from me, you *workers of lawlessness*" (modified NRSV; 7:23). The primary criterion for entrance into the kingdom of God, then, will not be the way in which one confesses Jesus or the powerful deeds one accomplishes but whether one has done God's will.

Doing the will of God entails living a life of righteousness. This is why Jesus teaches his disciples to pray, "Your will be done on earth as it is in heaven" (Matt 6:10) and defines his new family in terms of those who do the will of his heavenly Father (Matt 12:50). Jesus, of course, is the perfect example of one who does God's will (Matt 26:42), thereby exemplifying what it means to live a life of righteousness. In the parable of the two sons, he teaches that doing God's will is not a matter of *saying* that one will do God's will but of *doing* God's will (Matt 21:28-32).

In 7:21-23 Jesus identifies those who call him "Lord" and prophesy in his name but do not do God's will as "workers of lawlessness" (NRSV: "evildoers"). Instead of conforming themselves to God's law as taught by Jesus, they have become a law unto themselves. Their criterion for good and evil is what they determine, not what Jesus teaches. Their law is what pleases them, what is convenient for them, what is agreeable to them.

The structure of Jesus' ethic is different from the ethic of those who are lawless. Good and evil are not determined by personal preference for Jesus, but by God's will. What is right and what is wrong is not a matter of personal choice but of divine decree. The structure of Jesus' ethic as revealed in this section and throughout the Sermon on the Mount can be summarized in this way. People, like good and bad trees, bear fruit that corresponds to their innermost self. If they are like sound and healthy trees, they do God's will and bear the fruit of righteousness. If they are like rotten trees, they refuse to do God's will and bear the fruit of lawlessness. This ethic can be summarized in this way:

Good trees ⇨ good fruit ⇨ righteousness ⇨ doing God's will

Rotten trees ⇨ rotten fruit ⇨ lawlessness ⇨ doing evil

Whereas in the first part of his warning Jesus alerted his disciples to the danger of false prophets in their midst, here he warns them of the danger of self-deception: the illusion that all is well and that there will be no judgment. This is why the false prophets will be utterly amazed on the Day of Judgment when they are excluded from the kingdom of heaven. Having called Jesus "Lord" and performed mighty deeds in his name, they assume that all is well. They cannot imagine they will be excluded from the heavenly banquet. But this is precisely what will happen. They will be excluded from the kingdom because they have not practiced the righteousness of the kingdom; they have not done God's will.

Jesus' teaching is a warning to disciples of every age not to be lulled into self-complacency. It is possible to confess Jesus as one's Lord without doing what he commands. It is even possible to perform powerful deeds by invoking his name without doing his will. But none of this will be of any avail on the Day of Judgment when the criterion of judgment will be whether or not one has produced the fruit of righteousness by doing God's will. If prophets are those who bear God's word and interpret that word for the community, false prophets are those who fail to obey the word they bear. The church has experienced such prophets in every age and will encounter them in the future, but Jesus has provided his disciples with a way to recognize them: it is not what they say but what they do that counts. It is not the spectacular nature of what they do that matters but the extent to which they do God's will. Those who understand this are truly wise.

Doers of the Word (7:24-26)

Jesus concludes his great teaching on righteousness by returning to the theme of the two ways. This time, however, he provides his disciples with a simile rather than with a metaphor. His simile draws a comparison between two kinds of builders. One wisely builds his house on rock with the result that it is not swept away when the floods come. The other foolishly builds his house on sand with the result that it collapses and is utterly destroyed when the floods come. Speaking to those who have just heard his sermon, Jesus says that those who hear his words and do them are like the wise builder who built his house on rock, whereas those who hear his words but do not do them are like the foolish builder who built his house on sand. Jesus' concluding words, then, warn his disciples to be doers of the word rather than mere hearers of the word, a theme that the letter of James also develops.

> But be doers of the word, and not merely hearers who deceive themselves. For if any are hearers of the word and not doers, they are like those who look at themselves in a mirror; for they look at themselves and, on going away, immediately forget what they were like. But those who look into the perfect law, the law of liberty, and persevere, being not hearers who forget but doers who act—they will be blessed in their doing. (Jas 1:22-25)

Although people must hear the word of the gospel before they can embrace it, hearing the word is not sufficient. As Jesus' explanation of the parable of the sower illustrates, people hear the word in different ways. Some hear it without understanding (Matt 13:19). Others hear it with joy but then fall away when trouble or persecution arises (Matt 13:20-21). Still others hear the word but are distracted by worldly cares (Matt 13:22). Just hearing the word, then, is not enough. If hearing is to bear fruit, it must be accompanied by understanding, and understanding must lead to action. In the parable of the sower, Jesus teaches that it is those who understand the word who bear fruit (Matt 13:23). They understand the significance of what they have heard; they comprehend that they must be doers of the word. Because they understand the surpassing worth of the kingdom of God, they do all that it requires.

Jesus illustrates the importance of doing the word in the parable of the two sons (Matt 21:28-33). In that parable, a father tells his two sons to work in the vineyard. One son refuses to go, but he changes his mind. The other son says he will go, but he does not. When Jesus asks the religious leaders which of the two did the will of his father, they correctly respond the first son, for it is not a matter of what one says but of what one does. It is not a matter of being a hearer of the word, but of being a doer of the word.

The distinction that Jesus draws between the wise and foolish builders anticipates what he says in the parable of the wise and foolish virgins who wait for the bridegroom (Matt 25:1-13). Whereas the wise virgins provide for the bridegroom's delay by bringing extra oil for their lamps, the foolish do not. Like those who hear the word of God but do not do it, they wait for the bridegroom without extra oil for their lamps. Decoded, the parable can be read in this way: the foolish virgins (foolish disciples) did not meet the bridegroom (Christ) at his coming (the Parousia) with oil (deeds of righteousness) in their lamps. The parable of the ten virgins, then, illumines the simile of the two builders in this way: Just as those who are wise will meet the Lord with works of righteous on the day of his coming, so those who are wise will build their life on the foundation of Jesus' words by doing the righteousness they require.

The manner in which Jesus concludes his teaching emphasizes the importance of doing the righteousness he has described throughout the sermon. Those who hear the sermon must enter through the narrow gate of righteousness if they hope to find the way to life. They must beware of false prophets who call Jesus "Lord" but do not produce the fruit of righteousness in their lives. They must be doers of the word rather than mere hearers of the word lest they be swept away on the Day of Judgment. The powerful manner in which Jesus ends this sermon shows that he does not view it as an impractical ideal or an ethic for the few. The way of life he describes is the way in which disciples ought to live. But they cannot live in this way in isolation from each other. If they hope to produce the fruit of righteousness in their lives, they must live in a community of like-minded disciples who are doers of the word. What was true for Jesus' first disciples is true for disciples of every age. Those who practice the sermon as an individual ethic apart from a community of like-minded disciples will always be frustrated. They will always find it an impossible ideal. Those who live in community in light of the in-breaking kingdom of God, however, will find the strength to live the ethic Jesus presents here.

The Authority of Jesus' Word (7:28-29)

After Jesus finishes his sermon, Matthew notes that the crowds were "astounded" at his teaching, "for he taught them as one having authority, and not as their scribes." This reference to the crowd echoes Matthew's setting of the sermon: "When Jesus saw the crowds, he went up the mountain; and after he sat down, his disciples came to him" (5:1). These crowds are the great crowds from Galilee, the Decapolis, Jerusalem, Judea, and from beyond the Jordan that follow him because of the powerful deeds he performs on their behalf: miracles and exorcisms that proclaim the in-breaking of God' kingdom (4:23-25). Thus, even though the sermon is addressed primarily to the disciples, Jesus proclaims it in the hearing of the great crowds that follow him.

The crowds are astonished because Jesus teaches with an authority they have not experienced in the teaching of the scribes. Their "astonishment," however, is not a substitute faith, nor is it an expression of faith. The people of Nazareth, for example, were astonished by Jesus' wisdom and deeds, but they did not believe in him (Matt 13:54). The astonishment of the crowds, then, is an expression of their puzzlement at the authoritative way in which Jesus teaches rather than an expression of their faith in him.

Whereas the scribes teach with an authority that comes from faithfully handing on what has been handed on to them, Jesus teaches with an authority that comes directly from God. He does not repeat what he has learned. He does not teach because others have commissioned him. He is not a Pharisee, a scribe, or a priest. He has not learned what he teaches from a renowned teacher or rabbi. He teaches with an inner authority that is often questioned and misunderstood. When he comes to Jerusalem, for example, the chief priests and the elders of the people challenge him, "By what authority are you doing these things, and who gave you this authority?" (Matt 21:23). This question of authority is so central to this gospel that the Gospel of Matthew can be viewed as a conflict of authority between Jesus and the religious leaders: Who has the authority to speak for God? The astonishment of the crowds at the authority with which Jesus speaks indicates that this is not just another sermon. It is a sermon spoken with the authority that belongs to the Son of Man who has the authority to forgive sins (Matt 9:6). It is the authority of the one who says, "All authority in heaven and on earth has been given to me. Go therefore and make disciples of all nations, baptizing them in the name of the Father and of the Son and of the Holy Spirit, and teaching them to obey everything that I have commanded you. And remember, I am with you always, to the end of the age" (Matt 28:18-20). It is the authority of Israel's Messiah, the Son of God, the one in whom the Father is well pleased.

Although the crowds do not know the source of his authority, the disciples have begun to sense the origin of Jesus' authority, and this may be the reason why Matthew does not record their reaction to the sermon. Unlike the crowds that follow Jesus to see his mighty deeds, the disciples follow him because he has called them and they believe in him, even though they are still men of little faith. By their life with Jesus, they have begun to understand his unique relationship to God, which allows him to call God his Father. They have understood that he acts and teaches with an authority that comes directly from God rather than from learning and education, ordination or tradition. Jesus speaks from the depths of an intimate relationship to God. He speaks as the one who says, "All things have been handed over to me by my Father; and no one knows the Son except the Father, and no one knows the Father except the Son and anyone to whom the Son chooses to reveal him" (Matt 11:27). He speaks with the authority of the Son of God.

The crowds do not understand the source of Jesus' authority and will not be able to comprehend this authority until they believe in him as the one whom the Father sent into the world to inaugurate the kingdom. They may admire the beauty and power of the sermon, but they will never be able to embrace it until they become Jesus' disciples. What is true of the crowds is true for all who hear or read the words of this sermon today. One need not be a believer to appreciate their beauty and wisdom. One need not be a disciple to be amazed at the authority with which Jesus teaches. But if one is not a disciple, the sermon will always be a matter of wonder and amazement, something to be admired but not necessarily to be acted upon.

But for those who respond to the call of discipleship, the sermon takes on a new meaning. It is not something to be amazed at, but something to be lived. It is not an ethical ideal; it is the perfect measure of the Christian life. Those who are disciples are not amazed at the authority with which Jesus teaches because they confess that he is their Lord. They understand that his authority to teach derives from the source of all authority.

The Sermon on the Mount is not a new set of rules and regulations, as if Jesus were giving an alternate version of the Ten Commandments. It is an exposition of how we can and should do God's will. It calls disciples to a greater righteousness by summoning them to single-minded devotion to God. Its essential meaning is found in the words, "Be perfect, therefore, as your heavenly Father is perfect" (Matt 5:48). Be whole and entire, single-minded in your devotion to God. Avoid everything and anything that divides your allegiance and makes you a hypocrite.

Those who read the Sermon on the Mount again and again will eventually become intimate with its words and understand how to make moral decisions. They will understand that whatever calls into question their devotion and allegiance to God in Christ is evil, and whatever is done in wholehearted service to God in Christ is good. Yes, the authority with which Christ teaches is astonishing. It is more astonishing, however, that this teaching shows us how to be perfect as God is perfect.

Notes

1. Michael W. Holmes, *The Apostolic Fathers: Greek Texts and English Translations,* 3rd ed. (Grand Rapids, MI: Baker Academic, 2007), 344.

For Further Reading

Allison, Dale C. *The Sermon on the Mount: Inspiring the Moral Imagination*. Companions to the New Testament. New York: Crossroad, 1999.

Augustine, Saint. *Commentary on the Lord's Sermon on the Mount with Seventeen Related Sermons*. The Fathers of the Church 11. Washington: The Catholic University of America Press, 1951.

Bauman, Clarence. *The Sermon on the Mount: The Modern Quest for its Meaning*. Macon, GA: Mercer, 1985.

Benedict XVI, Pope. *Jesus of Nazareth: From the Baptism in the Jordan to the Transfiguration*. San Francisco: Ignatius, 2008.

Betz, Hans Dieter. *The Sermon on the Mount: A Commentary on the Sermon on the Mount including the Sermon on the Plain (Matthew 5:3–7:27 and Luke 6:20-49)*. Hermeneia. Minneapolis: Fortress, 1995.

Bonhoeffer, Dietrich. *The Cost of Discipleship*. Translated by R. H. Fuller. New York: Simon & Schuster, 1995.

Carson, D. A. *Jesus' Sermon on the Mount and His Confrontation with the World: An Exposition of Matthew 5–10*. Grand Rapids, MI: Baker, 2004.

Carter, Warren. *What Are They Saying about Matthew's Sermon on the Mount?* New York: Paulist Press, 1994.

Chrysostom, John. *Homilies on the Gospel of Matthew*. Nicene and Post Nicene Fathers 10. Grand Rapids, MI: Eerdmans, 1991.

Davies, W. D. *The Setting for the Sermon on the Mount*. Cambridge: Cambridge University Press, 1964.

Davies, W. D., and D. C. Allison. *The Gospel according to Matthew*. Vol 1. International Critical Commentary. Edinburgh: T. & T. Clark, 1988.

Dibelius, Martin. *The Sermon on the Mount*. New York: Charles Scribner's Sons, 1940.

Dumais, Marcel. *Le Sermon sur la Montagne: État de la rescherche Interpretation Bibliographié.* Paris: Letouzey et Ané, 1995.

Greenman, Jeffrey P., and Timothy Larsen, Stephen R. Spencer, eds. *The Sermon on the Mount through the Centuries: From the Early Church to John Paul II.* Grand Rapids, MI: Brazos, 2007.

Gregory of Nyssa: *Homilies on the Beatitudes,* Leiden: Brill, 2000.

Guelich, Robert A. *The Sermon on the Mount: A Foundation for Understanding.* Waco: Word, 1982.

Hendrickx, Herman. *The Sermon on the Mount: Studies in the Synoptic Gospels.* London: Geoffrey Chapman, 1984.

Jeremias, Joachim. *The Sermon on the Mount.* Philadelphia: Fortress, 1983.

Kinghorn, Kenneth Cain, ed. *John Wesley on the Sermon on the Mount.* Nashville: Abingdon, 2002.

Kissinger, Warren S. *The Sermon on the Mount: A History of Interpretation and Bibliography.* ATLA Bibliography Series 3. Metuchen, NJ: The American Theological Library Association, 1975.

Lambrecht, Jan. *The Sermon on the Mount: Proclamation and Exhortation.* Good News Studies 14. Wilmington, DE: Michael Glazier, 1985.

Lapide, Pinchas. *The Sermon on the Mount: Utopia or Program for Action?* Maryknoll, NY: Orbis Press, 1986.

Luther, Martin. *The Sermon on the Mount (Sermons) and The Magnificat.* Luther's Works. Vol. 21. Saint Louis: Concordia, 1956.

Luz, Ulrich. *Matthew 1–7: A Commentary.* Minneapolis: Augsburg, 1989.

McArthur, Harvey K. *Understanding the Sermon on the Mount.* New York: Harper & Brothers, 1960.

Pelikan, Jaroslav. *Divine Rhetoric: The Sermon on the Mount as Message and as Model in Augustine, Chrysostom, and Luther.* Crestwood, NY: St. Vladimir's Seminary Press, 2001.

Schnackenburg, Rudolf. *All Things Are Possible.* Louisville: Westminster John Knox, 1996.

Stanton, G. N. "Sermon on the Mount/Plain." In *Dictionary of Jesus and the Gospels,* edited by Joel B. Green, Scott McKnight, and I. Howard Marshall, 735–44. Downers Grove, IL: InterVarsity, 1992.

Strecker, George. *The Sermon on the Mount: An Exegetical Commentary.* Nashville: Abingdon Press, 1988.

Talbert, Charles H. *Reading the Sermon on the Mount: Character Formation and Decision Making in Matthew 5–7.* Columbia, SC: University of South Carolina, 2004.

Thomas Aquinas, Saint. *Summa Theologiae,* q. 69. In volume 24 (1a2æ. 68–70), *The Gifts of the Spirit,* translated by Edward D. O'Connor, 43–64. Cambridge: Cambridge University Press, 2006.

Windisch, Hans. *The Meaning of the Sermon on the Mount: A Contribution to the Historical Understanding of the Gospels and to the Problem of Their True Exegesis.* Philadelphia: Westminster, 1950.